Essential
Menorca

by Tony Kelly

Tony Kelly took up travel writing after
teaching English in Sudan and China.
He writes regularly for newspapers and
magazines, specialising in walking and
the outdoors. When not travelling he
lives near Cambridge with his wife and
young son. Among his other books are
AA *Essential Mallorca, Essential Costa
Brava* and Spiral Gran Canaria.

Above: *the beach at Cala Macarelleta*

AA Publishing

Above: *Plaça des Born, Ciutadella*

Find out more about AA Publishing and the wide range of services the AA provides by visiting our website at www.theAA.com

Written by Tony Kelly

First published 1998. Reprinted Jun and Nov 1998, Jun 1999.
Second edition 2000. Reprinted Feb, Aug and Oct 2000, May 2001.
Reprinted Apr 2002. Information verified and updated.

© Automobile Association Developments Limited 2002
Maps © 2002 Automobile Association Developments Limited

Published by AA Publishing, a trading name of Automobile Association Developments Limited whose registered office is Millstream, Maidenhead Road, Windsor, Berkshire SL4 5GD. Registered number 1878835.

A CIP catalogue record for this book is available from the British Library.

ISBN 0 7495 1632 1

Colour separation: BTB Digital Imaging Limited, Whitchurch, Hampshire

Printed and bound in Italy by Printer Trento Srl

Contents

About this Book

Essential *Menorca* is divided into five sections to cover the most important aspects of your visit to Menorca.

Viewing Menorca pages 5–14
An introduction to Menorca by the author.
> Menorca's Features
> Essence of Menorca
> The Shaping of Menorca
> Peace and Quiet
> Menorca's Famous

Top Ten pages 15–26
The author's choice of the Top Ten places to see in Menorca, each with practical information.

What to See pages 27–90
The main areas of Menorca, each with its own brief introduction and an alphabetical listing of the main attractions.
> Practical information
> Snippets of 'Did You Know…' information
> 5 suggested walks
> 3 suggested tours
> 2 features

Where To... pages 91–116
Detailed listings of the best places to eat, stay, shop, take the children and be entertained.

Practical Matters pages 117–24
A highly visual section containing essential travel information.

Maps
All map references are to the individual maps found in the What to See section of this guide.
For example, Fornells has the reference ✚ 29D4 – indicating the page on which the map is located and the grid square in which the village is to be found. A list of the maps that have been used in this travel guide can be found in the index.

Prices
Where appropriate, an indication of the cost of an establishment is given by **£** signs:
£££ denotes higher prices, **££** denotes average prices, while **£** denotes lower charges,

Star Ratings
Most of the places described in this book have been given a separate rating:

✪✪✪   Do not miss
✪✪   Highly recommended
✪   Worth seeing

Viewing
Menorca

Above: *boats at Fornells*
Right: *meditating at Cala d'Alcaufar*

5

Tony Kelly's Menorca

Stones and Wind
Mario Verdaguer called his novel about Menorca *Stones and Wind*, and it is easy to see why. The stones are everywhere, from prehistoric burial chambers to modern barns, often side by side in the same field. As for wind, of eight distinct named winds, the fiercest and most common is the *tramuntana*, the north wind which blows for around 60 days a year.

'Wind and stones', 'a rock strewn with earth' – Menorca has been called many things. 'The blue and white island', for the clarity of its light and the contrasts between dazzling white houses and a turquoise sea. 'An open-air museum', for its megalithic monuments – piles of ancient stones which blend into the modern landscape. Sometimes it is difficult to know where the clichés end and the truth begins.

Romans and Byzantines, British and Spanish colonists have all left their mark; even the tourist invasion since the 1960s has created its own monuments. But the biggest influence on Menorca remains what it has always been – the sea.

There are plenty of crowded beach resorts, indistinguishable from their equivalents elsewhere; yet at the same time you find peaceful coves, where pine-clad rocks surround arcs of fine sand. Out of season you might have one of these beaches to yourself. Yourself and the sharp north wind.

The cities at either end of the island personify Menorca's contrasts. Georgian Maó, the colonial capital, is a place of civil servants and naval officers, protected by one of the world's great harbours. Catalan Ciutadella, all aristocratic mansions and Gothic churches, is just 45km away but feels like another world. Between them is a rural landscape of meadows, cattle and drystone walls, punctuated by solid market towns and a gentle range of hills.

Even on the most crowded beaches you are never far from an unspoilt cove, such as this one at Cala Pregonda

Don't fool yourself; you would not be in Menorca if it wasn't for sun, sea and sand. But stick to the beach for a fortnight and you will never know what else you are missing.

Menorca's Features

Geography and Landscape

- Menorca is the second largest of the Balearic Islands, a group that includes Mallorca, Ibiza and Formentera.
- Menorca lies 225km southeast of Barcelona at the eastern extremity of Spain.
- Menorca measures 53km from east to west and 23km from north to south at its widest point.
- Menorca has 220km of coastline, with more beaches than all the other Balearic Islands put together.
- The highest mountain is Monte Toro (358m).
- Menorca has at least 1,000 prehistoric monuments and 15,000km of drystone walls.

Language

Most people speak Menorquín, which is a dialect of Catalan. Since 1983 Catalan and Castilian Spanish have both enjoyed official status on Menorca, but there has been a trend towards the revival of Catalan, especially in place-names. Menorquín contains a number of words inherited during the 18th-century British occupation – examples include *grevi* (gravy) and *winder* (a sash window).

The countryside is dotted with ancient monuments, like this 6th-century church at Torelló

Climate

- Menorca has an average daily maximum temperature of 20.3°C, rising to 28°C in July and falling to 14°C in January. Menorca has an average of 315 sunny days a year.
- Menorca is the wettest of the Balearic Islands; the rainy season is from October to April.

People

- Menorca has a population of 70,000, of whom around 22,000 live in Maó and 21,000 in Ciutadella.

Tourism

- In 1950 Menorca had 200 hotel rooms; by 1995 it had 40,000 in hotels and apartments.
- Menorca received 8,000 tourists in 1960, 200,000 in 1980 and 1.1 million in 2000 – 58 per cent were from Britain, 15 per cent from Germany and 16 per cent from Spain. A further 73,000 people visited on cruise ships.
- About 98 per cent of tourists arrive between April and October.

Essence of Menorca

Menorca is the quiet one of the Balearics. Mallorca may be larger, Ibiza may be brasher, but Menorca remains calm and dignified, confident of its own charms.

The wild olive trees of the north coast, bent into shape by the *tramuntana*, are symbolic of a people and an island shaped by history and a rugged landscape. Numerous invasions have not changed the Menorcan character – courteous and welcoming to strangers, yet self-sufficient and fiercely independent. Tourism has brought many benefits, but the Menorcans have not let themselves get carried away. The impression you get is of an island at ease with itself.

Arenal d'en Castell (below) and modern sculpture in Maó

THE **10** ESSENTIALS

If you only have a short time to visit the island, or would like to get a really complete picture of it, here are the essentials:

• **Take a boat trip** around Maó harbour (► 23), then stroll along the waterfront for a drink in Cala Figuera (► 33).

• **Make the pilgrimage** – on foot or by car – to Monte Toro (► 20), the hilltop convent at the centre of the island.

Sun, sea and sand – the Mediterranean dream

• **Wander the back streets** of Ciutadella, where every other house is the palace of a noble family, with hidden architectural details and coats of arms above the door (► 38–44).

• **Have lunch by the harbour** at Fornells (► 18) – *caldereta de langosta* (► 98) if you can afford it.

• **Walk to a remote beach** that cannot be reached by car – take a picnic and plenty of water, and settle down to your own private view.

• **Seek out** some of Menorca's prehistoric sites and try to unravel the mystery of the *taulas* (► 13).

• **Go to the trotting races** in Maó or Ciutadella at weekends (► 113), the best place to see Menorcans indulge their passion for horses.

• **Find out where** there is a festival going on (► 116) and drop everything to get there – especially if it is the Festa de Sant Joan in Ciutadella.

• **Try some Mahón cheese** (► 55), then buy some to take home.

• **Lie on the beach** soaking up the sun – everyone else does it at least once. But don't forget your sunblock.

The traffic-free streets in the centre of Maó are home to some of the smartest shops on Menorca

The Shaping of Menorca

About 100 million years ago
Menorca is formed by a geological fusion between fragments of continental Europe and Andalusia.

2,000–123 BC
The Talaiotic period produces burial caves, *navetas* and large settlements with *talaiots* and *taulas*.

400 BC
Carthaginian invaders enlist Balearic slingshot throwers to fight in the Punic Wars; they are paid in wine and women.

123 BC
Roman conquest; ~~norca~~ is named ~~Minor.~~ ~~is introduced,~~ ~~lished at~~ ~~uilt~~

AD 533
After a century of Vandal rule, Menorca becomes part of the Byzantine Empire.

902
The Balearic Islands enter the Caliphate of Córdoba, under Islamic rule. Ciutadella, Menorca's second town, becomes Medina Minurka.

Pirate Barbarossa – his name means 'red beard'

1229
Jaume I of Aragón conquers Mallorca. The Arab rulers agree to become his vassals, paying an annual tribute in wheat, cattle and lard.

1287
Alfonso III of Aragón lands at Maó and the Moors surrender. Christianity is restored. Alfonso divides Menorca up among his followers but dies in 1291 aged 25. Menorca is ruled by the kings of Mallorca and Catalan becomes the main language.

1349
The kingdom of Mallorca comes to an end and Menorca is incorporated into Aragón.

1492
Aragón unites with Castile and Granada to create modern Spain.

1535
The Turkish pirate Barbarossa attacks Maó; more than half the population are killed or enslaved.

1554
Construction of Fort Sant Felip.

1558
A Turkish raid on Ciutadella destroys most of the city.

17th century
The British gain treaty rights to the use of Port de Maó. British influence on Menorca grows and Maó becomes the main city.

1708
The British occupy Menorca in the name of Charles, Archduke of Austria.

1713
The Treaty of Utrecht confirms British rule. The capital is moved to Maó and a new road is constructed across the island.

1756
The Battle of Menorca ends in a French victory and the execution of the British Admiral Byng.

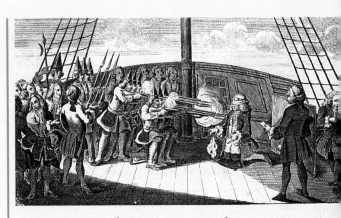

1763–82
The second British occupation under the Treaty of Paris and the building of Georgetown (Es Castell).

1782–98
Menorca returns to Spanish rule. Fort Sant Felip is destroyed.

1798
The British retake Menorca without loss of life.

1802
The Treaty of Amiens returns Menorca to Spain.

1854
Opening of a steamer service between Maó and Barcelona.

1909
Formation of a Society for the Attraction of Foreigners.

1936–9
The Spanish Civil War – Menorca remains staunchly Republican and is the last part of Spain to surrender to General Franco. Under Franco's dictatorship (1939–75), the use of the Catalan language is forbidden.

1953
The first charter flight from England lands in Menorca.

1969
The opening of Sant Climent airport leads to the tourist boom.

1975
Death of Franco and restoration of the monarchy.

1978
A new constitution grants limited autonomy to the Spanish regions.

Admiral Byng pays the price for the loss of Menorca in 1756

1983
The Balearic Islands become an autonomous region, with Catalan as an official language.

1988
A new coastal law prohibits any development within 100m of the sea.

1993
Menorca is declared a Unesco Biosphere Reserve; the aim is to protect the environment yet support traditional industries and tourism.

2000
As the number of visitors reaches one million, the Balearic government proposes an eco-tax on tourists.

Peace & Quiet

Camí de Cavalls
This bridleway around the entire Menorcan coast was first built in the 14th century and restored during the brief French occupation of 1756–63. It has mostly fallen into disrepair; ambitious plans to reopen the whole route have met with opposition from landowners and to date only a small section in the southeast has been reconstructed.

The Roman road to the summit of Santa Agueda gives spectacular views across the island

It's not difficult to find peace and quiet in Menorca – sometimes it's harder to get away from it. Even on the most crowded beaches, you are never more than a short walk away from a peaceful cove, fragrant pine woods or tranquil countryside. Go in winter and you have the island to yourself; only one tourist in 100 arrives between November and March. You might have to wrap up against the north wind, but winter and, especially, early spring are beautiful on Menorca, and the mild sunny days are perfect for walking.

Walking

The paths and minor roads that have criss-crossed Menorca since Roman times provide gentle walking on largely flat land. The biggest challenges are the hills of Monte Toro (► 20) and Santa Agueda (► 84), but even these can be managed by anyone who is reasonably fit. Other good areas are the limestone gorges of the south (► 16) and the numerous coastal paths. Walking in the countryside, you encounter an attractive rural landscape of Moorish farmhouses, curved olive-wood gates, sheep-shelters and drystone walls. Rights of way are not always clear and forbidding notices are not uncommon, but a word with the farmer will often help. Remember to shut all gates and not to walk over crops. Wherever you are walking, it is a good idea to carry water and food and to protect yourself from the sun.

Prehistoric Sites

Menorca's prehistoric sites are among the most peaceful places on the island. Most are situated in the midst of farmland and reached along minor roads; although they are on private land visitors have free, open access.

The most common monuments include *navetas*, burial chambers shaped like an upturned boat, and *talaiots*, large circular structures used as both dwellings and watchtowers. Most mysterious of all are the *taulas*, T-shaped 'tables' which probably performed some religious ritual function.

Spring flowers in the Algendar Gorge and the S'Albufera nature reserve

Birds and Flowers

Menorca is a popular staging-post for thousands of migrant birds each spring and autumn, pausing for rest on their way across the Mediterranean. The best sites for birdwatching are the S'Albufera marshes (► 24), the southern gorges and the wilder coastal areas. Endemic species include red kites and booted eagles, as well as the brightly coloured bee-eater, which nests in sandbanks and dunes. The cliffs, fields, gorges and woods of Menorca become a riot of wild flowers in spring; among more than 200 species are several varieties of orchid, which come into flower between March and May.

Menorca's Famous

Mateu Orfila (1787–1853)
Dr Mateu Orfila was born in Menorca but became Dean of Medicine at the University of Paris. He is known as the founder of modern forensic medicine after his ground-breaking work on toxicology in 1813. A bust of Dr Orfila stands outside his house in Carrer Ses Moreres, Maó.

Joan Pons (1946–)
The baritone Joan Pons was born in Ciutadella and still visits Menorca as often as time allows. Since 1980 he has performed at opera houses across Europe and North America, including La Scala in Milan, Covent Garden in London and the Metropolitan Opera in New York. In June 2001 he played Falstaff at the opening night of Maó's restored Teatre Principal (► 37)

Alfonso III of Aragón (1265–91)

Although he only spent 45 days on Menorca, the hero of the Reconquest can take most of the credit for the influence of Catalan culture on the island. Succeeding to the throne at the age of 20, he immediately set about planning to capture Menorca. He sailed from the mainland in 1286, reached Maó in January 1287 and conquered Menorca two weeks later. During his brief stay he established a system of government that was to last for several centuries; he also distributed land among his followers, earning the nickname 'the Liberal' since he rarely refused a request. He was capable of cruelty as well – those Moors too poor to pay a ransom and too weak to work as slaves were simply taken out to sea and drowned. Alfonso died in Barcelona at the age of 25; his statue, donated by General Franco, stands in the Plaça Conquesta in Maó.

Sir Richard Kane (1662–1736)

When the British arrived in Menorca, resistance to Protestant rule and resentment at the duplicitous nature of their conquest meant there was a need for a governor who would win Menorcans' respect. Richard Kane fitted the bill perfectly. A Northern Irish soldier who had served in Flanders and Canada, he arrived in 1713 to become Lieutenant-Governor. His first act was to build a road across the island, from Maó to Ciutadella, financed by a tax on alcohol – much of the road stands today. At the same time he moved the capital from Ciutadella to Maó. He drained marshes, planted orchards, introduced Friesian cattle, and made daily visits to the market in Maó to check on prices and measures. Agricultural production increased by five times in 40 years. Kane remained in Menorca until his death and was buried in Fort Sant Felip. He is remembered on Menorca with affection and a monument to his achievements stands near the start of the Camí d'en Kane (► 87).

This monument to the memory of Sir Richard Kane was erected by the Menorcan people in 1973

14

Top Ten

Above: *Naveta des Tudons*
Below: *sailing near Fornells*

1
Barranc d'Algendar
(Algendar Gorge)

✚ 28C3

🍴 At Cala Santa Galdana
(£–££)

🚌 Buses from Maó,
Ciutadella & Ferreries to
Cala Santa Galdana in
summer

↔ Cala Santa Galdana
(► 64)

❓ Conditions underfoot
vary greatly from
season to season, and
you may find locals
discourage you from
continuing.

*A dramatic limestone gorge, buzzing with
wildlife, which runs for 6km from Ferreries to
the south coast.*

Menorca's *barrancs*, or gorges, are wild and lonely places,
deep clefts formed over tens of thousands of years by the
gradual erosion of the limestone plateau in the south.

The gorges attract a huge variety of wildlife – birds,
butterflies, flowers. Kestrels and kites nestle among the
rushes; you see herons, buzzards and booted eagles.
Lizards sun themselves on the rocks and tortoises wade
through the marshes. The combination of rainfall, humidity
and protection from the wind produces a richness of
vegetation rarely seen elsewhere.

Algendar Gorge is the most dramatic of all – and one of
the most challenging to explore. The stream flows
throughout the year, opening out at Cala Santa Galdana

*The lush valley floor
supports orchards and
market gardens as well
as a huge variety of
wild flowers*

(► 64) into a wide river beside the beach. From here you
can walk part of the way along its western side, where
pine trees grow out of the cliffs at remarkable angles, but
the path is often overgrown.

There is also limited access at the northern end. Take
the minor road off the Maó–Ciutadella highway 100m west
of the Cala Santa Galdana exit; when the tarmac runs out
(after a half-hour walk), turn down the lane to your right.
You can walk a short way along the gorge before finding
your way blocked.

2
Cala Pregonda

A peaceful bay, backed by pine and tamarisk woods, in a remote and sheltered corner of the north coast.

✚ 28C4

🍴 None

↔ Binimel-là (➤ 52)

Everyone has their own favourite Menorcan cove but the one factor they all have in common is that you cannot reach them by road. Approaching Cala Pregonda on foot, you wonder what all the fuss is about – surely a perfect cove cannot have concrete houses behind the beach? But sit against the dunes with your back to the houses, surrounded by wild flowers on a quiet day in spring or autumn, looking out beyond the shore to the sandstone rocks and beyond that to Cap de Cavallería (➤ 69), and you begin to feel the magic of this place.

An old Roman road runs from Santa Agueda (➤ 84), but the easiest approach is from Binimel-là (➤ 52). Take the whitewashed steps over the wall at the west end of Binimel-là beach, follow the track across salt flats and a pebbly cove, climb a small headland above the dunes, then drop down to the beach.

The first sight of Cala Pregonda as you approach on foot from Binimel-là

The water is crystal-clear, ideal for swimming, though you might have to navigate your way around yachts. A short distance out to sea is a rocky islet with its own sandy beach, just right for a couple of families. Near here is Es Prego, the sandstone outcrop said to resemble a hooded monk (*prego* means proclamation), carved into shape by the fierce north wind. And behind the beach are the pine woods, the best place to take a picnic if you want to escape the crowds – and the sun.

And the houses? They were put up before the restrictions on coastal development were introduced. Even such modest building would not be permitted today.

3
Fornells

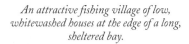

🕂 29D4

🍴 Wide choice of
restaurants on the
quayside (££–£££)

🚌 Buses from Maó

↔ Cala Tirant (➤ 65)

Torre de Fornells

🕐 Tue–Sat 11–2, 6–9; Sun
11–2

✋ Moderate

*Fornells – scenes from a
fishing village*

*An attractive fishing village of low,
whitewashed houses at the edge of a long,
sheltered bay.*

Fornells is everybody's idea of a Mediterranean fishing
village – white-painted houses around a harbour bobbing
with boats, restaurants on the waterfront along a palm-
lined promenade. Nowadays, of course, tourism is more
important than fishing, but there is still a fishing industry
here and the fish in the restaurants is genuinely local and
fresh. Fornells is known above all for its spiny lobsters, the
essential ingredient in a *caldereta de langosta* (➤ 98). King
Juan Carlos of Spain sails over regularly from Mallorca just
to eat lobster at Fornells.

The village is built on the west side of the Bay of
Fornells, close to the open sea. The natural harbour is 5km
in length, similar to that at Maó. The commander of the
first British invasion force to
Menorca wrote to his
superiors that Maó and
Fornells were the two best
ports in the Mediterranean.

Founded to defend the
north coast against pirate
ships, Fornells grew in impor-
tance in the 17th century with
the building of Castell Sant
Antoni, modelled on Fort Sant
Felip (➤ 76). The castle ruins
stand beside the sea, facing a
small island crowned by a
watchtower. A path from here
leads to the cape, where there
is a lighthouse, a small rock
shrine and another watch-
tower, Torre de Fornells,
opened as a museum. You can
climb to the top of the tower
to experience what would
once have been the view of
approaching invaders.

But most visitors don't go
to Fornells for history. They go
to soak up its simple beauty,
to walk beside the quay
then choose a harbourside
restaurant to enjoy the
freshest fish possible.

4
Monte Toro

✚ 29D3

☎ 971 37 50 60

🍽 Sa Posada (££) and café (£)

✋ Free

↔ Es Mercadal (➤ 72)

❓ First Sun in May – blessing of the fields

The spiritual and physical high point of Menorca – a hilltop convent right at the centre of the island.

Menorca's highest mountain (358m) is crowned by a convent which has become an important centre of pilgrimage. Its name almost certainly derives from *al-tor*, Arabic for 'highest mountain', despite the local legend about a bull (*toro* in Spanish) who discovered a statue of the Virgin in a cleft in the rock.

Get there by driving or walking the twisting 3km road from Es Mercadal; an alternative approach on foot is to follow the track between two white posts at the entrance to San Carlos farm, 1km out of Es Mercadal on the Camí d'en Kane (➤ 87). The simple courtyard is peaceful and attractive – an old well, an olive tree, a 16th-century stone tower, a low white-washed refectory. You enter the church through a pretty porch with several arches and dozens of potted plants. Even when you get inside the 17th-century Renaissance church, there is little adornment – a plain white dome, tapestries on the walls, a 1943 altarpiece with a statue of the Virgin with the legendary bull at her feet. This is La Verge del Toro, the chief focus of pilgrimage. Mass is said here at 11AM each Sunday and the bishop holds a service each May to bless the island's fields.

A large statue of Christ welcomes weary pilgrims arriving at the summit of Monte Toro

From the terrace and car park there are sea views on all four sides. Look down from the terrace over neat vegetable and herb gardens which are tended by the community of nuns who still live on Monte Toro.

5
Naveta des Tudons

The oldest roofed building in Spain – a Bronze Age burial chamber recently restored to its former glory.

Of all the prehistoric monuments on Menorca, this is probably the most visited. Until the 1950s it was dishevelled and overgrown; for centuries it had been used as a cattle-shed but was fully restored in 1959–60 and again in 1975.

The word *naveta* describes a burial chamber, built in the shape of an upturned boat. Most are horseshoe-shaped in design, with a low, narrow entrance at the straight end and a small ante-chamber leading into the main burial chamber. Some, like this, were built on two storeys; the bodies were left to decompose upstairs and the bones were subsequently transferred to the ground floor ossuary. Excavations in the 1950s revealed at least 100 corpses in Naveta des Tudons, some with bronze bracelets still around their arm-bones.

✚ 28B4

✉ On Maó–Ciutadella road, 4km from Ciutadella

🕐 Free access

🍴 None

↔ Torre Llafuda (➤ 89)

Navetas are unique to Menorca – of around 45 remaining, this is in the best condition. It is 14m long, 6m wide and around 4m high. Although a notice warns you not to disturb the stones by climbing, you can enter the *naveta* on hands and knees for a close look at the main chamber, supported by stone columns. You may even think you can smell the bones.

Because it is on the main road so close to Ciutadella, Naveta des Tudons attracts a large number of visitors. Come here early in the morning or late in the afternoon to catch some of the atmosphere and history of this place.

Menorca's Bronze Age burial chambers were built using limestone from local quarries

6
Plaça des Born, Ciutadella

🕂 28A4

🍴 Wide choice of restaurants & bars (£–££)

🚌 Buses from west coast resorts to Plaça de S'Esplanada in summer; buses from Maó arrive 5 minutes' walk away

↔ Ciutadella (► 38)

❓ Festa de Sant Joan 23–24 Jun

Open-air cafés and elegant 19th-century buildings – one of the finest city squares in Spain.

During the Fascist era this square at the heart of Ciutadella was renamed after General Franco, but everyone continued to call it 'es Born'. The word *born* means parade-ground – the square was used for jousting contests in earlier times and is still the venue for an equestrian parade during the city's annual festivities in June.

At the centre of the square is an obelisk commemorating those citizens of Ciutadella who were killed or abducted into slavery during the Turkish raid of 1558. Much of Ciutadella was destroyed, including the *alcázar* or governor's palace. The crenellated town hall, with its

Plaça des Born – sit down, order a coffee and watch the world go by

Moorish-looking row of palms standing guard, was built in the 19th century on the same site. Peep inside to see the panelled ceilings, portraits of local worthies and the Gothic chamber on the first floor.

Across the square are two 19th-century palaces, those of the Torre-Saura and Salord families, built symmetrically to either side of Carrer Major del Born. Their neo-classical façades are dominated by Italianate loggias; the ground floors facing the square are given over to gift shops and cafés. Near by is the 19th-century theatre, and the adjoining coffee-house, Cercle Artistic, with harbour views.

Opposite: the houses of Maó seem to grow out of the harbour walls

7
Port de Maó (Maó Harbour)

The glory of Maó – a deep, natural harbour that has protected the Menorcan capital throughout its history.

When the European powers fought over Menorca in the 18th century, the greatest prize was the harbour at Maó. The world's second largest natural harbour, 5km long and up to 900m wide, was wrongly believed to provide an impregnable Mediterranean base.

The best way to see the harbour is on one of the one-hour boat tours that leave from the foot of the harbour steps in summer. The water is deep but it remains incredibly clear and from a glass-bottomed boat you can see the sea bed.

From the water you get the best views of the 18th-century houses lining either side. High on a cliff between Maó and Es Castell is the Hotel del Almirante, a plum-red Georgian villa that was the home of the British Admiral Collingwood. Facing it on the north shore is Sant Antoni (Golden Farm), where Nelson is said to have stayed in 1799.

Between Maó and the harbour entrance are three islands. The first, Illa del Rei (King's Island), was the first place to be 'liberated' by Alfonso III; when the British built a hospital here, it was known as 'Bloody Island'. Next comes Illa Plana (Flat Island), a former quarantine island; this function was taken over in 1900 by the largest island, Lazareto, whose high walls were designed to prevent infections from reaching Maó. South of Lazareto, at the entrance to the harbour, are the ruins of Fort Sant Felip (► 76); to the north is the headland of La Mola, the most easterly point in Spain.

🕂 29F2

🍽 Waterfront restaurants at Maó & Es Castell (££–£££)

🚌 Buses between Maó & Es Castell

⛴ Boat tours of the harbour from Maó & Es Castell in summer

↔ Maó (► 30), Es Castell (► 70), Fort Sant Felip (► 76)

8
S'Albufera des Grau

🕇 29E3

🕐 Free access to national park

🍴 At Es Grau (£–££)

🚌 Buses from Maó to Es Grau in summer

↔ Shangri-La (➤ 85)

A protected wetland area close to the east coast that acts as an important refuge for aquatic birds.

There used to be many more areas of wetland around the Menorcan coast, but most were drained for agriculture by the British or reclaimed for tourist *urbanizacións* in the 1960s. Of those that survive, S'Albufera is the largest and most important. A 70-ha lagoon is separated from the sea by a barrier of sand, creating salt-water marshes beside a freshwater lake.

The shores of the lake are a peaceful spot to stroll, with bird-watching hides and a boardwalk trail. In winter there are migrant colonies of osprey and booted eagles; in spring and autumn the lake attracts waders and wildfowl. Species regularly seen here include cormorants, herons, spoonbills and terns. You may also spot turtles, toads and snakes.

The lake is separated from the beach at Es Grau by pine woods and dunes. Es Grau is an old-fashioned seaside village, with fishing boats in the harbour and white houses down to the water's edge. The large beach is perfect for children as the water is shallow all the way out to Illa d'en Colom, seen across a channel 400m out to sea.

In summer you can take boat trips to the island, where there is a choice of sunny or shady beaches. This is the largest of Menorca's offshore islands; there is evidence of early habitation, with Roman ruins and a Byzantine church. The island, home to a protected species of lizard, is now part of the S'Albufera Park, the focus of Menorca's Biosphere Reserve.

S'Albufera is at the centre of the Unesco Biosphere Reserve on Menorca

9
Son Bou

*A long stretch of fine sandy beach
with marshes, caves and an early
Christian church.*

 29D2

 Bars & restaurants
(£–££)

Much of the south coast is made up of small, indented coves; Son Bou could hardly be more different. The longest beach on Menorca, it has almost 3km of pale golden sand, a sunbather's dream with facilities from beach bars to water-skiing and windsurfing. The water shelves gently and swimming is generally safe, but there are occasional dangerous currents so you should look out for the red and green flags. The beach is so long that it rarely gets crowded; it is always possible, especially at the western end, to find your own secluded spot.

 Buses from Maó to Son Bou & Club San Jaime in summer, plus a shuttle 'train' connecting the hotels to the beach

Torre d'en Gaumés (► 26)

At the east end of the beach, beneath two ugly hotels, is one of Menorca's more remarkable ancient monuments – a 5th-century Christian basilica, discovered in 1953. Similar to North African churches of the same period, it has three naves divided by pillars and a huge font, carved from a single stone. When you realise how long it lay hidden beneath the sand you wonder what further treasures are still waiting to be uncovered.

In the cliffs above the basilica are some large prehistoric burial caves, used as summer houses by Menorcan families. Climb up to these caves for the best views over the beach. Above the west end of the beach, separated by marshland, is the purpose-built resort of Sant Jaume Mediterrani. This has everything you could want for a family holiday – pools, shops, discos, plus the popular Club San Jaime with its water-chutes and labyrinthine maze.

*Son Bou – a perfect
beach for families*

25

10
Torre d'en Gaumés

29D2

Free access

None

Son Bou (➤ 25)

An atmospheric abandoned village with impressive Bronze Age monuments and views over the south coast.

The extensive prehistoric settlement of Torre d'en Gaumés contains several well-preserved Talaiotic buildings. Most of it dates from around 1400 BC, though there is an even older sepulchre near by and evidence of habitation until Roman and perhaps medieval times.

Get there by following the signs from the Alaior-Son Bou road. As soon as you leave this road, the three *talaiots* are visible in the distance, 2km away down a country lane. A paved road leads around the site, making this the one prehistoric site in Menorca which is accessible to wheelchairs and pushchairs, though the path is bumpy in places and there is no access to the *taula* precinct.

Besides the three *talaiots*, there is a *taula* whose horizontal stone has collapsed, enabling you to appreciate its design, with a carefully hollowed-out centre to fit on top of the vertical stone. (It is possible that the hollow was enlarged at a later date for use as a Roman sarcophagus.) Near by is the best-preserved example of a hypostyle chamber, a roofed building with columns, possibly used as a dwelling but more likely as a sheep shelter or grain store. There is also an ingenious water storage and filtration system, probably Roman, with channels dug into the rock beneath a large flat surface.

A glimpse of an ancient culture – the remains of the prehistoric village of Torre d'en Gaumés

This is a peaceful spot, with wild flowers growing among the ruins and views stretching from Monte Toro (➤ 20) to the south coast.

What To See

Above: *Cala Macarelleta*
Right: *a roundabout with a difference, outside Ciutadella*

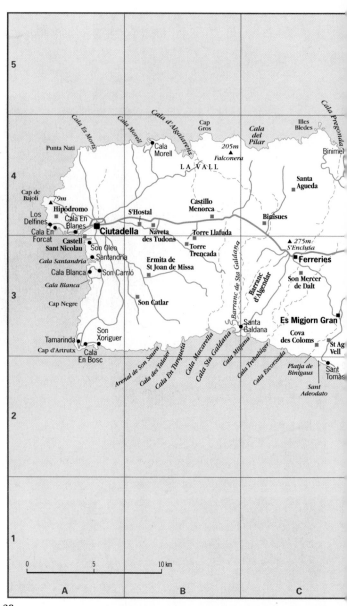

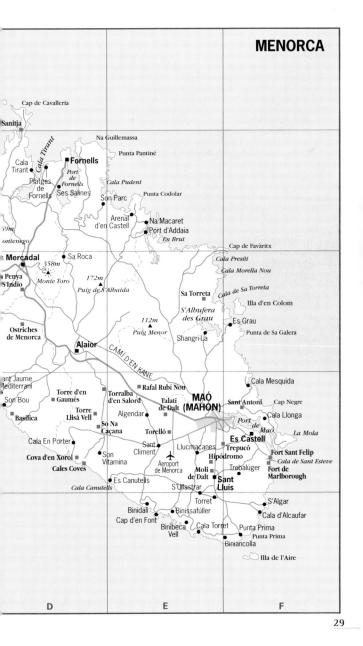

MENORCA

Cap de Cavalleria

Sanitja

Cala Tirant

Na Guillemassa

Fornells

Punta Pantiné

Cala Tirant

Port de Fornells

Platges de Fornells

Ses Salines

Cala Pudent

Son Parc

Punta Codolar

Arenal d'en Castell

Na Macaret

Port d'Addaia

En Brut

Cap de Favàritx

59m

ontenego

Mercadal

Sa Roca

Cala Presili

Cala Morella Nou

358m

Monte Toro

Penya S'Indio

172m

Puig de S'Albaida

Sa Torreta

Cala de Sa Torreta

Illa d'en Colom

S'Albufera des Grau

112m

Puig Menor

Es Grau

Punta de Sa Galera

Ostriches de Menorca

Alaior

CAMÍ D'EN KANE

Shangri-La

ant Jaume lediterrani

Son Bou

Torre d'en Gaumés

Torralba d'en Salord

Rafal Rubí Nou

Cala Mesquida

Torre Llisà Vell

Talatí de Dalt

MAÓ (MAHÓN)

Sant Antoni

Cap Negre

Basílica

Algendar

So Na Caçana

Cala Llonga

Port de Maó

La Mola

Cala En Porter

Torelló

Sant Climent

Llucmaçanes

Es Castell

Cova d'en Xoroi

Son Vitamina

Aeroport de Menorca

Trepucó

Hipódromo

Fort Sant Felip

Cala de Sant Esteve

Cales Coves

Molí de Dalt

Trebalúger

Fort de Marlborough

Es Canutells

S'Ullastrar

Sant Lluis

Cala Canutells

Torret

S'Algar

Binidalí

Binissafúller

Cap d'en Font

Binibeca Vell

Cala Torret

Cala d'Alcaufar

Punta Prima

Punta Prima

Biniancolla

Illa de l'Aire

D   E   F

Maó

You cannot separate Maó from its harbour – without it, the city would not be there. The harbour is the reason why the great powers fought over Menorca for so long; it is the reason why the British moved the capital to Maó in 1722.

The best way to arrive in Maó is by boat, sailing into the harbour past its various islands and watching as the city appears, 25m up on the cliff face, a jumble of attractive white-washed houses which seem to grow out of the old sea walls. Ferries from Barcelona, cruise ships and naval vessels, luxury yachts and even the odd fishing boat share space in the deep, clear waters and the narrow waterfront road is lined with restaurants and bars. Come here on a summer evening, when the buzz of conversation is echoed by the water, and you will understand how Maó is still, more than anything else, a city by the sea.

> *'June, July, August and Maó are the best ports in the Mediterranean.'*
>
> ANDREA DORIA
> Genoese admiral (1468–1560)

Maó

There was a city here in Roman times; its name, Magón, may be that of Hannibal's brother but is more likely derived from a Phoenician word meaning 'shelter'. Modern Maó dates from the Catalan conquest; it was Alfonso III, the conqueror, who began both the Church of Santa Maria and the city walls, of which only the gateway of Port de Sant Roc survives.

Alfonso III, the founder of modern Maó: his statue stands in Plaça Conquesta

The greatest influence on the city you see today, though, is probably British. It was the British who moved the capital to Maó and filled it with Georgian-style architecture not seen anywhere else in Spain. Streets such as Carrer Isabel II are adorned with grand 18th-century houses, with furniture in the style of Sheraton and Chippendale and bow-windows (*boinders* in local language) leaning across the pavement.

For three centuries Maó (which is frequently still referred to by its Spanish name, Mahón) has had to serve its foreign rulers, whether British, French or Spanish. The result is a city that is serious rather than stylish, industrious rather than flamboyant. At times its status as a capital makes it feel like a much bigger city; at other times, when work is done for the day and everyone greets everyone else by name during the evening *passeig* across the Plaça de S'Esplanada, it feels like little more than a small village.

What to See in Maó

The town hall contains the records of a city going back almost 2,000 years

AJUNTAMENT (TOWN HALL) ✪

Mao's town hall was built in 1613 but completely refashioned in 1788 with the addition of an English clock, a gift from the first British governor Sir Richard Kane. A stone stairway leads to the portico, where plaques record the completion of the original building, together with royal visits and coronations. Also here is a sculpted image of Saint Sebastian, patron saint of Maó. The lobby is lined with portraits of former governors, including the Count of Lannion (the first French governor) and the Count of Cifuentes, the first Spanish governor following British rule. A watercolour by the Italian painter Giuseppe Chiesa shows French troops attacking Fort Sant Felip in 1756. Near here is the municipal debating chamber, with velvet armchairs for the deputies, wooden benches for the public and a gallery of portraits of 'illustrious Menorcans'.

ATENEU ✪

For a city with the population of a small provincial town, Maó has a rich intellectual tradition, perhaps a result of the exposure to so many foreign cultures and ideas. The real focus of Mao's intellectual life is this scientific, literary and artistic association, founded in 1905. Visitors are welcome to see the collections of maps, ceramics, watercolours and fossils. This is a museum like museums used to be, kept open by devoted scholars.

CALA FIGUERA ✪✪

Take the long stairway which leads from the city centre down to the waterfront, turn right by the ferry station along the Moll de Llevant, and after about half an hour, as the road bends to the right, you enter the deep cove of Cala Figuera. This is the fashionable area of Maó – the *club marítimo* is here, the city's best hotel is up on the cliff and there are restaurants ranging from fresh fish to pizza and up-market *nouvelle cuisine*. Sitting in the lunchtime sun, you have a perfect view of the Illa del Rei in the middle of Maó harbour. Once known as 'the English creek' because English boats would moor here for fresh water, it is now – controversially – the storage site for Menorca's petrol reserves. There is a long-standing plan to move the tanks across the harbour to the naval base to create more space at Cala Figuera for a marina and avoid the need for petrol tankers to disfigure the lunchtime scene on the waterfront.

COLLECCIÓ HERNÁNDEZ MORA ✪

Joan Hernández Mora (1902–84) was a local historian, author and teacher who devoted much of his spare time to collecting historic documents and artefacts in order to preserve his beloved Menorcan heritage. When he died childless, he left his collection to the city of Maó and it has been turned into this small museum in the cloisters of the Església del Carme (► 34). The chief part of the display comprises furniture and books; there is also a fascinating collection of maps.

🔲 34C2
🍴 Lots of restaurants (££–£££)
🔁 Port de Maó (► 23), Es Castell (► 70)

Above: *by the harbour at Cala Figuera – the place to see and be seen*

🔲 34C2
✉ Claustre del Carme
☎ 971 35 05 97
🕐 Mon–Sat 10–1
🍴 Near by (£–££)
🎟 Free
🔁 Església del Carme (► 34)

33

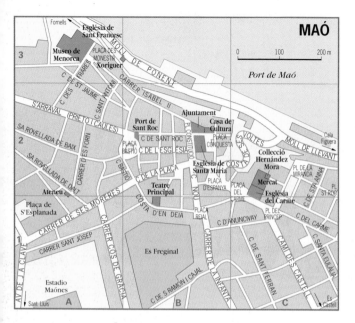

MAÓ

Port de Maó

✚ 34C2
✉ Plaça del Carme
☎ 971 36 24 02
🍴 Near by (£–££)
✋ Free
🔄 Collecció
   Hernández Mora
   (➤ 33)

ESGLÉSIA DEL CARME ✪✪

This massive baroque church was built in 1751 as a Carmelite convent but extensive damage during the Spanish Civil War means that most of what you see is heavily restored. The stern façade leads to a bright interior with bare stone walls and arches and a vaulted ceiling. During the original building of the church, a Roman necropolis was discovered in the vaults, along with various coins and urns which are now in the Museu de Menorca (➤ 36). Next to the church, the cloisters of the convent have been turned into a covered shopping mall that incorporates Maó's main market, as well as a super-market in the basement. This is a good place to buy Mahón cheese, cured hams and local sausages. Folk-dancing displays are held here on Thursday evenings in summer.

The bare stone walls of Església del Carme were designed to make it harder to attack

A Walk Around Maó

Begin in Plaça de S'Esplanada (➤ 36) with your back to the barracks and take Carrer Ses Moreres in the right-hand corner. Head down this street, noting the bust of Dr Orfila (➤ 14) outside No 13.

Continue into another shopping street, Costa de Sa Plaça, which drops sharply to Plaça Constitució. Turn right into Carrer Nou; this brings you to Plaça Reial. Turn left to reach Plaça del Carme. Cross this square diagonally to look into the cloistered market then head down the steps to the fish market in Plaça d'Espanya.

You could drop down to the waterfront here – but to continue your city walk, follow the stone railings around the square into Plaça Conquesta, with its statue of the Conqueror, Alfonso III. The narrow alley off the square to the right gives a splendid view of the harbour.

Leave Plaça Conquesta diagonally opposite where you entered to return to Plaça Constitució. Turn right by the town hall then bear left into Carrer Isabel II, whose Georgian houses back on to the harbour walls.

The road ends at the Museu de Menorca (➤ 36).

Turn left to enter a maze of narrow streets and whitewashed houses. Another left turn, then right, brings you to Carrer Sant Antoni, emerging beside an old convent, now an art gallery. Turn left to reach Pont de Sant Roc, the only remaining section of the city walls. Turn right into Plaça Bastió and cross this square to enter Carrer d'Alaior. Turn right at the end to return to Plaça de S'Esplanada.

Distance
3km

Time
1 hour

Start/end point
Plaça de S'Esplanada
🚉 34A1
🚌 Buses from all over the island terminate here

Lunch
Café Marès (£)
✉ Plaça de la Conquesta
☎ 971 36 95 76

Plaça de S'Esplanada, where the walk begins and ends, is the best place to see the people of Maó at play

34A3
- ✉ Plaça des Monestir
- ☎ 971 35 09 55
- 🕐 Apr–Oct: Tue–Sat 10–2, 5–8; Sun 10–2. Nov–Mar: Tue–Sat 10–1, 5–7; Sun 10–1
- 🍴 Near by in Plaça Bastió (£–££)
- 💷 Inexpensive

Opposite: *Santa Maria is the closest thing Maó has to a cathedral*

34A1
- 🍴 Lots of restaurants & cafés (£–££)
- 🚌 Buses to Maó from across the island terminate here
- ↔ Ateneu (➤ 32)
- ❓ Market Tue, Sat

Menorca's largest museum is housed in the cloisters of a former monastery

MUSEU DE MENORCA ✪✪✪

Come here after exploring Menorca's archaeological sites to discover what happened to all the finds and to piece together the missing links in your knowledge of Menorcan history.

Coins, pottery and funerary objects from several different cultures are gathered under one roof, together with the island's largest collection of fine arts. Among the objects on display is a complete skeleton of *Myotragus balearicus*, a goat-like mammal that once lived on Menorca but became extinct with the arrival of man. There are Talaiotic sculptures, Roman mosaics and the British coat of arms from Fort Sant Felip (➤ 76).

The setting, in the cloisters of the old Franciscan monastery, is a delight, with galleries arranged around a shady courtyard with an old well at its centre.

PLAÇA DE S'ESPLANADA ✪✪

This esplanade – the square between the barracks and the streets of the old town – is the best place to go to see the people of Maó at play. There are pigeons and palm trees, fountains and flower beds, a bowling alley and a children's playground which is busy from late afternoon until dusk. Old men sit in the shade reading newspapers; teenagers queue for popcorn and ice-cream.

On Tuesdays and Saturdays there is an open-air clothes market here; on Sundays, street entertainers join the crowds. During Maó's festivals Plaça de S'Esplanada acts as an outdoor venue for concerts and parties. The square is lined with cafés – a good place to come during the evening *passeig* to sit with a drink, feeling the pulse of Maó.

PORT DE MAÓ (MAÓ HARBOUR ➤ 23, TOP TEN)

SANTA MARIA ⭐⭐

Maó's main church was begun soon after the Catalan conquest, then rebuilt in neo-classical style in the 18th century in a gesture of defiance to the island's British, Protestant rulers. Everything here is done on a massive scale. A huge, forbidding façade, like a great ochre cliff-face broken only by the incongruous presence of four sash windows, leads through the entrance portal to a long, single nave. Most people come here to see (or hear) the organ, built by the Swiss maker Johann Kyburz and imported from Barcelona during the Napoleonic Wars with the help of the British. During the summer there are daily concerts of organ music.

🚩 34B2
✉ Plaça Constitució
☎ 971 36 39 49
🍴 Near by in Plaça Bastió (£–££)
🎫 Free (organ concerts – moderate)
↔ Ajuntament (➤ 32)
❓ Organ concerts Jun–Oct: Mon–Sat 11AM

TEATRE PRINCIPAL ⭐⭐

When the Greek community was forced out of Maó in the late 18th century, the former Orthodox church was converted into a dance hall; when that outgrew its usefulness, this theatre was built instead. Designed by a Florentine architect and full of Italianate touches, it was the first opera house in Spain when it opened in 1829. The theatre was comprehensively restored and reopened in 2001.

🚩 34B1
✉ Costa d'en Deià 46
☎ 971 35 57 76
🍴 In Plaça Reial (£)

XORIGUER ⭐

Menorca's leading gin distillery promotes itself as a tourist attraction in order to entice customers in. In practice all you get to see is the shop, with a few copper stills bubbling away behind glass. The good news, though, is that you can drink as much as you like – not just gin, but herbal liqueurs ranging from camomile to carob. Another speciality is *calent*, made with aniseed, cinnamon and saffron and served warm to clients 'on the house' by bar owners in Ciutadella each Christmas.

🚩 34B3
✉ Moll de Ponent 93
☎ 971 36 21 97
🕐 Summer: Mon–Fri 8–7; Sat 9–1. Winter: Mon–Fri 9–1
🍴 On the waterfront (££–£££)
🎫 Free
↔ Port de Maó (➤ 23)

Ciutadella

Where Maó is bureaucratic, Ciutadella is artistic; where Maó has power, Ciutadella has style. The nobility and the church stayed behind when the capital was moved to Maó with the result that Ciutadella remains a pure Catalan city, undiluted by British or French architecture or the ideas that colonial rulers brought in their wake.

There were Carthaginian and Roman settlements here, and the Arabs made it their capital, but Ciutadella, Menorca's second town, reached its zenith in the 17th century when the island's richest families settled here.

Wander the maze of narrow streets fanning out from the cathedral, their Gothic palaces each marked by a coat of arms carved above the door; sit beneath the palm trees in the Plaça des Born at dusk; join the citizens of Ciutadella for their annual festival, when richly caparisoned horses prance through the streets, and you begin to appreciate the truth of the Count of Cifuentes' *bon mot.*

> *'Maó may have more people, but Ciutadella has more souls.'*

COUNT OF CIFUENTES
Governor of Menorca (1782)

What to See in Ciutadella

CASTELL SANT NICOLAU ✪

This 17th-century octagonal defence tower, with drawbridge, moat and turrets, stands alone on a limestone platform halfway around the Passeig Maritim (► 42). Nowadays it is used as an exhibition centre, with displays on environmental themes and occasional art exhibitions. The real reason for coming here, though, is to watch the sun set over the sea and see the mountains of Mallorca appear, silhouetted against a pink sky. It is beautiful and romantic, but you won't be alone.

- 28A4
- Passeig Marítim
- Mon–Sat 11–1, 6–8 in summer
- None
- Free
- Passeig Marítim (► 42)

CATEDRAL ✪✪

Ciutadella has been Menorca's religious capital since Arab times; when Alfonso III conquered the island in 1287, one of his first acts was to have the main mosque reconsecrated as a church. The Catalan-Gothic structure took shape over the next 75 years, though part of the old mosque still remains in the ramp of the north tower, reminiscent of an Islamic minaret. The church finally gained its cathedral status in 1795, when a bishopric was restored to Ciutadella after an absence of 1,300 years.

Outside, a stark, windowless wall – probably added after the Turkish raid on Ciutadella in 1558 – leads to thick square buttresses. Inside, an aisleless nave leads to a pentagonal apse and a dozen side chapels. Most of the interior fittings were destroyed during the Spanish Civil War and what you see is heavily restored – a plaque in the floor pays tribute to Bishop Pascual Marroig, who restored the cathedral between 1939 and 1967.

- 28A4
- Plaça de la Catedral
- 971 38 07 39
- Daily 8–1, 6–9
- Near by (£–££)
- Free
- Plaça des Born (► 22), Museu Diocesà (► 40), Museu del Pintor Torrent (► 41), Palau Salord (► 42), Ses Voltes (► 44)

Ciutadella's harbour is lined with fashionable fish restaurants, where the fish comes straight off the boat

MOLÍ DES COMTE ✪

First built in 1778 for the Count of Torre-Saura, this windmill fell into disrepair until it was restored in the 1960s by the present Count; it was opened to the public in 1994. You can climb the steps for a close-up look at the machinery and a view of the city's rooftops through the sails. Beneath the windmill, the old granary has recently been converted into a smart shopping arcade, Centre d'Artesania, with shops selling local crafts, clothes and sandals, as well as Menorcan sausages, wine and cheese.

MUSEU DIOCESÀ ✪

The Museum of the Diocese of Menorca is housed in a former Augustine monastery close to the cathedral. Peaceful baroque cloisters lead on to a series of rooms containing ecclesiastical treasures including vestments, chalices and reliquaries. There is also a room devoted to prehistoric finds, and a collection of paintings by the Catalan artist Pere Daura, born in Ciutadella in 1896.

Behind the museum, in Plaça de la Libertat, is the city's lively food market, with stalls selling fresh fruit, vegetables, meat, cheese and fish.

> ### Did you know ?
>
> *The palm-lined Plaça Alfons III, opposite the windmill, was formerly the gateway to Ciutadella – and the pedestrian street beyond, which begins as Carrer de Maó and leads to Plaça des Born, was the city's main thoroughfare. The gateway was demolished in 1868 when the city walls were torn down to create what is now the ring road Sa Contramurada.*

Above: *the tower of the Diocesan Museum*

Opposite: *3,000 years of Menorcan history can be traced at the Municipal Museum*

MUSEU MUNICIPAL ⊕⊕

The Bastió de Sa Font was built as a fortress in the late 17th century; it was subsequently used as a grain store, a gas factory and a water tank before being fully renovated and opened as the city's museum in 1995. The displays, neatly laid out in a long, bright, vaulted gallery, are carefully captioned and there are leaflets available in English to help you to find your way around.

🞤 28A4
⊠ Bastió de Sa Font
☎ 971 38 02 97
⊙ Tue–Sat 10–2
🍴 In city centre (£–££)
♿ Inexpensive
↔ Santa Clara (➤ 44)

The museum tells the history of Menorca from pre-Talaiotic to Muslim times through a collection of fascinating exhibits gathered from archaeological excavations around the island – bone knives which go back 3,000 years, ancient spears and slingshots, Roman coins, jewellery, oil-lamps and dice. The most gruesome display case contains a collection of Iron Age skulls, which show that the Talaiotic culture had developed advanced techniques in cranial pathology. As well as head wounds caused by blows from weapons, there are fractures which are the result of trepanning, or surgery. Signs of scarring show that the patient survived the operation and made a full recovery.

MUSEU ⊕
DEL PINTOR TORRENT

José Torrent, a native of Ciutadella who was born in 1904, is widely considered one of the two greatest Menorcan painters of the 20th century – the other is Joan Vives Llull, from Maó. After his death in 1990, a number of Torrent's works were gathered together in an old town house close to the Plaça des Born. You can follow his development from youthful Impressionism to the Expressionism of his final years, and see for yourself why he is known as 'the Van Gogh of Menorca'.

🞤 28A4
⊠ Carrer Sant Rafel 11
☎ 971 38 04 82
⊙ Mon–Sat 11–1, 7:30–9:30 in summer
🍴 Near by (£–££)
♿ Free
↔ Plaça des Born (➤ 22), Catedral (➤ 39), Palau Salord (➤ 42)

41

28A4
Carrer Major del Born 9
Apr–Oct: Mon–Sat 10–2
In Plaça des Born (£–££)
Inexpensive
Plaça des Born (➤ 22),
Catedral (➤ 39), Museu
del Pintor Torrent (➤ 41)

*Palau Salord is typical of
the noble mansions
which dominate the old
town of Ciutadella*

PALAU SALORD ✪✪

The streets of the old city are filled with 17th–century palaces, built by Menorca's aristocratic families when they moved to Ciutadella from their country estates. Most are still owned by the original families, in some cases the descendants of those who were rewarded in 1287 when Alfonso 'the Liberal' divided up his new conquest among his followers and friends.

Peep into any of these palaces when the doors are open and you see fine courtyards with stone stairways, Italianate loggias and galleried arcades. Most, including the Torre-Saura palace on Plaça des Born and the Martorell palace on Carrer de Santíssim, are closed to the public; for a glimpse of aristocratic living you have to visit the Palau Salord on the Plaça des Born. Among the riches on display are antique furniture, tapestries and oil paintings, gilded mirrors and a frescoed ballroom.

28A4
In the harbour (££–£££)
Plaça des Born (➤ 22),
Castell Sant Nicolau
(➤ 39)

PASSEIG MARÍTIM ✪✪

This wide promenade, completed in 1997, follows the seafront around the peninsula from the small beach at Cala des Degollador to the marina. This is the place to come at dusk to watch the sun set over the sea and join the locals on their evening *passeig*. Mothers and grandmothers, teenagers holding hands – the whole population of Ciutadella seems to be there. As the promenade approaches the city centre, a flight of steps leads down to the port where you can walk around the harbour and look up above the old city walls to the Plaça des Born.

PLAÇA DES BORN (➤ 22, TOP TEN)

A Walk Around Ciutadella

Begin in Plaça des Born (➤ 22) with your back to the town hall.

Go up Carrer Major del Born, directly facing the obelisk. Turn left in front of the cathedral along Carrer Ca'l Bisbe.

This takes you past the bishop's palace to Palau Squella, a fine 18th-century mansion.

Turn left at the end of the street, then right into Carrer Sant Rafel, passing the Museu del Pintor Torrent (➤ 41) and continuing into Carrer Sant Miquel. At the first crossroads, a narrow passage on the left leads to the old sea walls.

Look down on to Pla de Sant Joan, a large open space that is the venue for the city's main festival in June (➤ 116).

Turn right to reach the old fort, now the Museu Municipal (➤ 41), then turn right on to Carrer Portal de Sa Font. Passing the convent of Santa Clara (➤ 44), continue along the narrow street ahead then turn left into Carrer Sant Antoni to reach Plaça Nova.

Ahead, Carrer de Maó leads to Plaça Alfons III, a popular meeting-place and a good lunch stop.

Turn right along the ring road, then right again into Carrer Alaior. When you reach the market turn right, then left into Carrer del Socors and left again into Carrer Seminari, an elegant shopping street. At the end of this street turn right then right again into Carrer del Roser. When you reach the cathedral, turn left to return to Plaça des Born.

This walk can be combined with a pleasant stroll along the Passeig Marítim (➤ facing page). Leave Plaça des Born on its southwest side to reach Plaça de S'Esplanada, a shady square of pine trees also known as Plaça dels Pins. From here you can drop down to the seafront promenade and follow it to its end. Return to Plaça de S'Esplanada along Carrer de Mallorca. Allow an extra hour.

Distance
2km

Time
1 hour

Start/end point
Plaça des Born
➕ 28A4

Lunch
Aurora (££)
✉ Plaça Alfons III 3
☎ 971 38 00 29

The back streets of Ciutadella seem designed for strolling

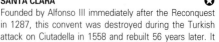

➕ 28A4
✉ Carrer Portal de Sa Font
☎ 971 38 27 78
🕐 Daily 6–1:30, 4:30–8:30
🍴 Near by (£–££)
🎟 Free
↔ Museu Municipal (➤ 41)

*Detail from the convent
of Santa Clara*

➕ 28A4
🍴 Lots of restaurants &
bars (£–££)
↔ Catedral (➤ 39), Museu
Diocesà (➤ 40)

SANTA CLARA ✪

Founded by Alfonso III immediately after the Reconquest in 1287, this convent was destroyed during the Turkish attack on Ciutadella in 1558 and rebuilt 56 years later. It was destroyed again during the Spanish Civil War and the building you see today dates from 1945. It is still a working convent and only the church is open to visitors; it is plainly decorated with white stone arches and the kaleidoscopic altarpiece, with its dazzling rainbows and purple skies, comes as quite a shock.

SES VOLTES ✪✪

This pedestrian alley at the heart of the old city, also named after the local historian José-Maria Quadrado, is the focal point of Ciutadella's social life. This is where café life reigns, as people spend their *siesta* sitting on canvas chairs in the shade of Moorish-style arches, then return during the evening *passeig* for a drink outside one of the bars on Plaça Nova before checking out the row of billboards to see what is on at the cinema.

> ### Did you know ?
>
> *Santa Clara was at the centre of a diplomatic incident in 1749 when three young women fled the convent and placed themselves under the protection of their British boyfriends, who were soldiers in the nearby garrison. The British governor, General Blakeney, refused to hand them back, but to satisfy the church authorities he had the room in which they were staying sealed by a priest each night. Eventually the three sets of lovers were allowed to marry. One of the neighbouring streets is still called Que No Passa – nobody shall pass.*

A Drive From Ciutadella to Maó

The map of Menorca is dominated by one road, the C721 connecting Maó to Ciutadella. A drive along the length of this road passes three inland towns and several prehistoric sites.

Start on the edge of Ciutadella, at the round-about with the sculpture of a prancing horse.

Pass the football stadium and the industrial estate on your left, with factory shops competing for your attention. After 4km the car park for Naveta des Tudons (➤ 21) is reached on the right; shortly after this there are more turn-offs to Torre Trencada (➤ 90) and Torre Llafuda (➤ 89). After 9km, skirt a crest by Castillo Menorca where you will have your first view of the central mountains.

After passing the manor house of Binisues (➤ 52) on your left, a series of bends takes you up to Ferreries (➤ 74). The road continues to Es Mercadal (➤ 72), with Monte Toro (➤ 20) dominating the view.

Shortly after bypassing Es Mercadal, Camí d'en Kane (➤ 87) leads off to the left; next you climb a twisting hill to a picnic area overlooking the rock formation known as Sa Penya de S'Indio, because of its apparent resemblance to an Indian brave. From here the road bypasses Alaior (➤ 48), then goes fast and straight to Maó.

Keep straight ahead at the industrial estate, following signs for 'Centre Ciutat'. Bear right at the mini-roundabout to reach Plaça de S'Esplanada, the start of the walk around Maó (➤ 35).

You can return to Ciutadella the same way, or combine this with one of the other drives (➤ 51 and 87). Alternatively, take the pretty country roads between Es Mercadal and Ferreries via Es Migjorn Gran (➤ 73).

Distance
44km one way

Time
1 hour

Start point
Ciutadella
🚩 28A4

End point
Maó
🚩 29E2

Lunch
Molí des Racó (££)
✉ Carrer Vicario Fuxà 53, Es Mercadal
☎ 971 37 53 92

Ferreries, Menorca's highest town

Around the Island

Outside the two cities, Menorca's attractions fall into three main categories, and to get a complete picture of the island you need to visit them all. There are the small inland towns, all of which reward an hour or two's gentle strolling. There are the prehistoric sites, more than a thousand in all, of which the most important are found in an area south and east of Alaior. Finally there is the coast, which is never far away – from huge modern resorts with all facilities to deserted coves where pine-fringed cliffs lean into the sea.

The two halves of Menorca came together 100 million years ago. The north, or *tramuntana*, is all dark soil and slate; its craggy coast, scarred by the north wind, is broken by deep inlets and stony beaches backed by dunes. The south, or *migjorn*, is milder and more sheltered, a low limestone plateau riven with gorges that spill into the sea along beaches of fine sand.

> *'All its life, its history, its landscape, even the idiosyncrasies of its inhabitants, are closely influenced by the sea.'*
>
> REV FERNANDO MARTÍ CAMPS
> *History of Menorca* (1971)

What to See Around the Island

+ 29D3

🍴 Bars & cafés; The
Cobblers restaurant (££)

🚌 Buses from Maó &
Ciutadella

↔ Torralba d'en Salord
(➤ 89)

❓ Market Mon, Thu; Festa
de Sant Llorenç Sun
following 10 Aug

ALAIOR ✪✪

Menorca's third largest town, 12km west of Maó, was founded by Jaume II of Mallorca in 1304 when he divided the island into seven regions, each with a central market town. The existence of Roman roads around the town, and the wealth of prehistoric remains near by, suggest that it was a centre of population much earlier.

There are few specific sights in Alaior, but it makes a pleasant place to stroll – a town of gleaming white houses huddled together in narrow streets which lead up to the parish Church of Santa Eulàlia at the town's summit. Jaume II built the first church here; it was later fortified by villagers following the Turkish attacks on Maó and Ciutadella. The present baroque church dates from the 17th century.

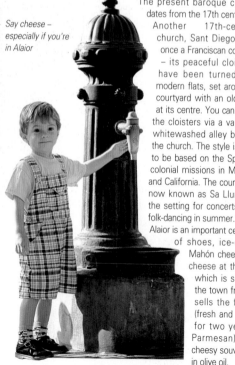

Say cheese – especially if you're in Alaior

Another 17th-century church, Sant Diego, was once a Franciscan convent – its peaceful cloisters have been turned into modern flats, set around a courtyard with an old well at its centre. You can enter the cloisters via a vaulted, whitewashed alley beside the church. The style is said to be based on the Spanish colonial missions in Mexico and California. The courtyard, now known as Sa Lluna, is the setting for concerts and folk-dancing in summer.

Alaior is an important centre for the manufacture of shoes, ice-cream and especially Mahón cheese (➤ 55). You can buy cheese at the Coinga factory shop, which is signposted as you enter the town from the south. The shop sells the full range from *fresco* (fresh and soft) to *añejo* (matured for two years and as strong as Parmesan), as well as various cheesy souvenirs and jars of cheese in olive oil.

ARENAL D'EN CASTELL

This popular holiday centre is the most westerly of the trio of resorts reached by heading north from Alaior. Each of the three has its own distinct character and Arenal (the name means 'sandy place') is the brash one. The setting is superb – a near-circular bay with a long arc of fine sand backing on to dunes and pine-fringed cliffs – but it is rather spoilt by the presence of two enormous modern hotels towering over the beach. There is windsurfing and water-skiing; you can hire pedal boats, motorboats, parasols and sunbeds. The shallow water and the presence of a first-aid post make this a safe beach for children.

🔢 29E4
🍴 Several bars & restaurants (£–££)
🚌 Buses from Maó & Fornells in summer
↔ Na Macaret (➤ 77), Port d'Addaia (➤ 78)

Arenal d'en Castell – lovely beach, shame about the rest

ARENAL DE SON SAURA

One of Menorca's prettiest beaches is also one of the hardest to reach. To get there by car you have to cross farmland and in summer the farmer levies a toll; this is one of the last remaining beaches where the island government has not yet managed to buy up the land in order to create free access. If you don't want to drive, you can walk from Cala En Turqueta (1 hour) on the coastal footpath from Son Xoriguer to Cala Santa Galdana. It is worth the effort – two long stretches of white sand, hidden behind fragrant pine woods and neatly divided by a woody outcrop. There are no beach facilities even in summer, so take a picnic.

🔢 28B3
🍴 None
⛴ Boat trips from Ciutadella & Cala En Bosc in summer
↔ Son Catlar (➤ 86)

49

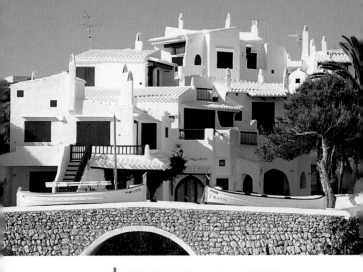

BARRANC D'ALGENDAR (► 16, TOP TEN)

BINIBECA VELL ●●●

🕂 29E1
🍴 Several bars & restaurants (££)
🚌 Buses from Maó in summer

A new coat of whitewash for Binibeca Vell (above)

You'll either love or hate this place – it is difficult to feel anything in between. To some it is an example of tasteful tourist development, based on architectural beauty and local style; to others it is tacky, artificial and ugly. One of the earliest coastal developments in Menorca, it was designed to resemble a Mediterranean fishing village, with whitewashed houses, orange trees and sun-drenched patios filled with geraniums. A maze of narrow alleys, Moorish archways, boats and sea views, it would be stunning if only it were authentic. The first giveaway is the name – would a real fishing village be called *Poblat de Pescadors* ('Fishing Village')? Then there are the notices for 'reception' and 'public relations', and the signs asking people to be quiet. Look beneath the steeple for the village church and you find an alcove with a crucifix inside – the architect needed a church for the postcards but the temporary 'villagers' have no need of a real one.

You could easily spend your whole holiday here – there is a supermarket, souvenir shops, restaurants and bars, swimming pools, squash courts, a children's play area and a car hire office in case you should want to see Menorca. The nearest beach is 1km away at Binibèquer – here you can hire sunshades, loungers and pedal boats and have lunch at a simple wooden shack which claims to be the only place in Menorca where you can drink with your feet in the sea.

A Drive Around the Southeast

This drive takes in Menorca's only stretch of coast road.

Start in Maó, leaving Plaça de S'Esplanada along Avenida Josep Anselm Clavé, passing the football stadium and following signs to Sant Lluís. Go through Sant Lluís (▶ 83) and over the roundabout towards the coast. After 1km, take the right fork to Punta Prima and after another 1km – when you see a satellite mast ahead – fork left, climbing a hill and dropping down to the sea. As you enter Punta Prima (▶ 79), a right turn at the first roundabout takes you on to the coast road.

Follow this road for 4km, passing some rocky coves before reaching Binibèquer beach for lunch. Another 1km takes you to Binibeca Vell (▶ 50). After exploring the village, turn right, left and left again at the next roundabout to bypass Binibeca Vell and return to the sea. As the road runs out – go left at the T-junction and swing wide left at the three-way intersection to return to the coast.

Eventually the road turns inland once more across a rocky landscape, followed by gentle countryside on its way to Sant Climent (▶ 83).

Turn left through the village on to the Cala En Porter road; after 4km, just past the turn-off to Cales Coves, take the country road to Alaior on your right.

You cross a typical landscape of meadows and drystone walls, as well as passing some interesting prehistoric sites.

On reaching Alaior (▶ 48), turn right and return to Maó on the main road.

Distance
48km

Time
2 hours plus lunch

Start/end point
Maó
✚ 29E2

Lunch
Los Bucaneros (££)
✉ Binibèquer beach
☎ No telephone
🕐 May–Oct only

Stop off in Alaior to wander the narrow streets

51

28C4
Bar/restaurant (£)
Cala Pregonda (► 17)

BINIMEL-LÀ ✪

Getting to Binimel-là is an adventure in itself. Head north from Es Mercadal along a series of country roads, then follow a wide dust track signposted to Binimel-là. After about 1½km the track forks left to drop down to the beach, where you can park your car beside a freshwater lake.

The beach, backed by sand dunes, is of red sand and pebbles; the water is deep and the absence of shade means you are exposed to the sun and wind. To escape this, head for the smaller sheltered beaches around the bay, popular with nudists – you can get there by ignoring the left fork mentioned above. The best reason for coming to Binimel-là, though, is in order to walk to Cala Pregonda (► 17).

28C4
Off the C721
Maó–Ciutadella highway at 31km
971 37 37 28
Apr–Oct: daily 11–7
Restaurant (££)
Moderate
Ferreries (► 74), Santa Agueda (► 84)

BINISUES ✪

This stately home on the road to Santa Agueda, just west of Ferreries, has been turned into an exhibition of traditional Menorcan life, customs and furniture. The home of the Salort y Martorell family, it retains its original furnishing and paintings, as well as farm buildings filled with old-fashioned tools. The top floor has interesting exhibitions of mounted butterflies, insects and birds, many of them endemic to Menorca. The name of the house, like so many in Menorca, reveals the island's Moorish past – *bini* is Arabic for 'sons of'. The restaurant here specialises in traditional Menorcan country cooking and seafood dishes.

The furniture at Binisues shows how wealthy Menorcan families used to live

CALA BLANCA ⭐

This pretty pine-fringed cove, just 4km south of Ciutadella, has been blighted in recent years by excessive development. Once there was just a small beach nestling between low limestone cliffs; now it has been engulfed to such an extent that the beach is a mere speck on the map of the 'village'. The beach is overlooked by several restaurants, all competing to attract families with facilities ranging from swimming pools and water slides to games rooms and 'adult entertainment'. At the back of the beach are the remains of a Bronze Age *naveta*.

🔢 28A3
🍴 Several restaurants & bars (££)
🚌 Buses from Ciutadella in summer
↔️ Cala Santandría (▶ 65)

CALA D'ALCAUFAR ⭐⭐

This small creek, 4km southeast of Sant Lluís, is classically Menorcan – fishermen's cottages reach down to the water's edge and the narrow, curving, sheltered inlet is lined with boats and backed by a sandy beach. This was the site of Menorca's first tourist hotel and it is still a popular weekend trip for the people of Sant Lluís. From the beach you can easily climb on to the cliffs, where a short walk leads to a headland crowned by a Martello tower – beneath which are two grottoes that can be entered by boat.

Cala d'Alcaufar was the site of the first British landing on Menorca, in 1708. Just to the north is S'Algar, reached by a separate road or on a recently restored section of the coastal bridleway, Camí de Cavalls. The development here is a lot less restrained and the slopes leading down to the sea are a jumble of villas and apartments.

🔢 29F1
🍴 Bar/restaurant beside the beach (£)
🚌 Buses from Maó in summer

Above: *Cala d'Alcaufar is one of Menorca's smallest and prettiest resorts*

53

Food & Drink

Menorca's cookery is rooted in its history. The Arabs introduced almonds, the Spanish brought peppers from America, while the British imported Friesian cattle, still used in today's dairy industry – but the essential ingredients remain truly Mediterranean: garlic, tomatoes and olive oil.

Seafood

Menorca's island cuisine relies heavily on the products of the sea. Most notable – and expensive – are spiny lobsters from Fornells, used in the classic soup *caldereta de langosta* (▶ 98). Fresh prawns and mussels are abundant; other fish includes mullet, sole and sea-bass. Squid is a speciality, stuffed with its own meat; vegetables such as aubergines and peppers are also frequently stuffed with seafood. A true *paella*, from Valencia, consists of saffron rice cooked with meat and fish, but its Menorcan equivalent, *arroz marinera*, is based on seafood. Other rice dishes include *arroz caldoso*, a fish and rice stew.

Mayonnaise
There are numerous legends as to the origins of mayonnaise (*salsa mahonesa*), but the most common has it invented by the Duc de Richelieu's housekeeper during the French occupation of Maó (Mahón). A blend of raw egg, olive oil and a touch of vinegar or lemon juice, it is usually mixed with garlic to make *allioli* and served with fish, rabbit or vegetables.

Meat Dishes

Meat – which could be beef, veal, pork or lamb – is often served roasted with *salsa de grevi* (gravy), a legacy of the British occupation. Menorcans are proud of their various sausages, a by-product of the winter *matança* or slaughter of pigs. The best-known are *sobrasada*, made of minced raw pork with hot peppers, and *botifarró* (blood pudding); others include *carn i xua*, *cuixot* and *salsitxa*. Order a *surtido de fiambres* (plate of cold cuts) and you might get all of these, along with cured ham and Mahón cheese (see opposite).

Detail of a number of attractively packaged local Mahon cheeses, displayed for sale in the Coinga factory shop in the old market town of Alaior

Tapas

Tapas (▶ 94) include octopus, snails and tripe but two of the simplest snacks are *tortilla*, a cold potato omelette, and *pa amb oli*, bread rubbed with tomato, sprinkled with olive oil and topped with ham or cheese. Bakers sell *formatjades* and *empanadillas*, small pies filled with sausage, cheese, tuna or spinach, as well as *bocadillos* (filled rolls).

Café society rules in Ciutadella

Desserts

La Menorquina ice-creams, from Alaior, are sold throughout Spain – as well as ice-creams and sorbets they produce a large range of frozen desserts, from *bikini* to *tarta de whisky*. Sweet biscuits are another local speciality, especially *amargas* and *carquinyols* (almond macaroons), while *ensaimadas* are fluffy, spiral pastries made with lard and dusted with sugar. *Cucusso* is made from honey, raisins and almonds.

Cheese

Cheese has been produced on Menorca since the 14th century and *queso de Mahón* is now one of Spain's leading cheeses, with its own *denominación de origen*. Until recently a seasonal farmhouse cheese, it is now produced industrially from pasteurised milk and exported across the world. Made in square loaves and cured for up to two years, its yellow rind is coated with oil as it matures. Varieties range from *tierno*, eaten mild and young and used to stuff Christmas turkeys, through *semi-curado* and *curado* to the fully mature *añejo*.

Drinks

There is only one wine producer left in Menorca and most wine is imported from mainland Spain. The best reds come from Rioja, made with the *tempranillo* grape and aged in oak. *Cava* is a sparkling wine from Catalunya. Beer is available everywhere – for draught beer, ask for *una caña*. Tap water is safe to drink but everyone drinks mineral water – *agua con gas* is sparkling, *sin gas* is still.

Gin

Gin, a spirit flavoured with juniper berries, was already produced in Menorca before the 18th century but its popularity with British sailors helped to modernise its manufacture. The leading producer is Xoriguer on Maó's waterfront, whose gin is sold in characteristic earthenware bottles called *canecas*. *Pomada*, gin with lemonade, makes a refreshing *apéritif* – though nowadays you're just as likely to see Menorcans ordering a Scotch on the rocks.

Above: *the absence of a beach means that Cala de Sant Esteve has remained peaceful and uncrowded*

Fort Marlborough
☎ 971 36 04 62
🕐 May–Oct: Tue–Sat 10–1, 5–8; Sun 10–1. Nov–Apr: Tue–Sun 10–1
👋 Moderate

CALA D'ALGAIARENS ✪✪✪

These twin beaches on Menorca's remote northwest coast are reached by crossing the fertile La Vall region until you reach a pair of gateposts surmounted by offputting 'private' signs. In winter you are within your rights to drive on; in summer the landowner levies a toll, justified by the need to restrict traffic pollution in this environmentally sensitive area.

Once through the gates, follow signs to *'playa'* and when the track runs out, walk through the woods – a haven for migrant bee-eaters in spring and summer – to reach the sea. The main beach is a wide horseshoe of golden sand backed by dunes – you can scramble over the low rocks to reach a second beach, Platja d'es Tancats. Both beaches shelve gently into the sea and offer safe bathing in sheltered waters. This is a lovely, peaceful spot which only really gets busy at summer weekends. There are no facilities.

CALA DE SANT ESTEVE ✪✪

St Stephen's Creek is named after an early Christian martyr whose remains were said to have been buried here. A deep, narrow inlet at the mouth of Maó harbour, it is mainly notable for its two military fortifications. On one side are the ruins of Fort Sant Felip (➤ 76); on the other, reached by a tunnel, the seven-sided **Fort Marlborough**, built by the British in the late 18th century. Unlike Fort Sant Felip, Fort Marlborough was never destroyed; it has recently been renovated and opened as a museum. This is great fun, but not for those of a nervous disposition – the special effects include explosions in the underground tunnels. You can climb up to the rooftop for more peaceful views.

CALA DEL PILAR ✪✪

This is a wild, lonely, beautiful spot which nevertheless gets busy at weekends with locals trying to escape the crowds. Get there by leaving the main Maó to Ciutadella road from the 34km point beneath the Castillo Menorca factory shop; when the tarmac road runs out, you pass through some gates on to farmland and park in a thick grove of oak and pine. Walk for 20 minutes through the woods and you emerge on to reddish dunes; from here you can scramble down to the beach, or over the headland to the next cove. The woods reach almost to the beach and even the dunes are covered in vegetation. This is a conservation area and notices in several languages remind you to keep the beach clean.

✚ 28C4
🍴 Beach bar in summer (£)

A sandy path leads through the woods to Cala del Pilar

CALA EN BLANES ✪

The coastline to the west of Ciutadella was once a succession of small beaches and pretty coves; now Cala En Blanes, along with its neighbours Cala En Bruc, Cala En Forcat and Cales Piques, have been swallowed up and merged into one continuous stretch of 'urbanisation', based around the busy tourist complex of Los Delfines. This is as close as Menorca gets to the mass tourist developments of the Spanish *costas*, with signs in English and German, villas in fake local style, overcrowding in summer and a complete absence of life in winter. At the heart of the resort, **Aquapark** is Menorca's first waterpark, with waterslides, soft play areas and crazy golf for the kids.

✚ 28A4
🍴 Bars & restaurants (£–££)
🚌 Buses from Ciutadella
↔ Ciutadella (► 38)

Aquapark
☎ 971 38 82 51
🕐 May–Oct: daily 10:30–6
💰 Expensive

57

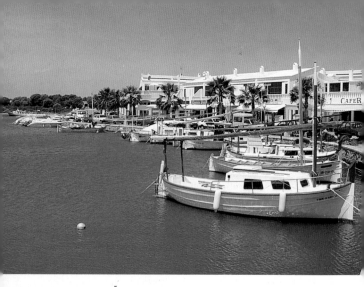

➕ 28A3
🍴 Wide choice of restaurants (££)
🚌 Buses from Ciutadella in summer

Above: chic and cheerful – Cala En Bosc

➕ 29D2
🍴 Bars & restaurants (£–££)
🚌 Buses from Maó in summer

CALA EN BOSC ⭐

Just 9km south of Ciutadella and easily reached on a fast road, Cala En Bosc has become one of Menorca's most fashionable resorts. Life revolves around the marina, built on the site of a drained wetland, and lined with trendy restaurants and bars. Small boats can enter the marina through a narrow channel; this is also a departure point for cruises to the remoter coves along the south coast. The neighbouring resort of Son Xoriguer, with its large twin beaches, is a centre for watersports, with schools offering windsurfing, water-skiing, scuba-diving and sailing. Both resorts are heavily developed and not for those seeking peace and quiet.

CALA EN PORTER ⭐⭐

One of Menorca's earliest beach resorts has grown into a major holiday centre. The setting is lovely – a wide beach leading to a narrow cove where almost unbelievably turquoise water shimmers between tall limestone cliffs. A *barranc*, or ravine, enters the sea via the marshland at the back of the beach. The western side is totally undeveloped, with cliffs tumbling into the sea; the eastern side must once have have been the same but the cliffsides are now covered with villas and terrace bars. The most unusual bar is Cova d'en Xoroi, a succession of stairways and rock platforms set in a natural cave high in the cliff-face with dramatic views over the bay and out to sea.

> ### *Did you know ?*
>
> *Xoroi was a legendary Berber pirate who was shipwrecked at Cala En Porter. He abducted a local girl and kept her in his cave for 10 years, during which time she produced four children. When his footprints in the snow gave him away the girl was rescued by her family and Xoroi threw himself into the sea.*

CALA EN TURQUETA ★★★

This beautiful spot could easily be destroyed by thoughtless development; as it is it remains blissfully unspoiled. The reason, as with so many of Menorca's beaches, is that it cannot be reached by road. Following a government campaign to reclaim Menorca's beaches, there is now a free car park – but it is still a 10-minute walk down to the beach and the gates are locked at 6PM.

Pine-covered cliffs look down on to clear blue water and a beach of soft white sand backs on to extensive pine woods. The beach itself shelves gently into the sea, making it ideal for swimming. For the best views, climb on to the western cliffs – the path here continues to the next cove, Cala des Talaier, and from there to Arenal de Son Saura (► 49).

🚌 28B3
🍴 None
🚤 Boat trips from Cala En Bosc & Ciutadella in summer
🔄 Ermita de Sant Joan de Missa (► 70)

CALA ESCORXADA ★★

You used to be able to reach this cove by the coastal footpath from Sant Adeodato (► 82) but the path has become a casualty of the ongoing battle between landowners and the authorities over rights of way. By Spanish law, everyone has access to the coast; the problem arises when you need to cross private land to get there. The owner of the land behind Cala Escorxada has denied access to ramblers by erecting barriers. The result is that the cove has become even more remote than it was and all the more attractive for those who do get there – either in a boat or by a long (two hours minimum) and difficult walk from Cala Santa Galdana (► 64). Cala Escorxada is typical of the south coast – limestone cliffs, pine woods and a semi-circular beach of soft white sand; it is also good for snorkelling.

🚌 28C3
🍴 None

Head for Cala En Turqueta to escape the crowds – although even here you will not be entirely alone

CALA MACARELLA ✪✪✪

A hike of around 30 minutes from the west end of Cala Santa Galdana (► 64) across a fragrant headland covered with wild flowers and herbs is followed by a steep, rocky descent to this delightful cove where a *barranc* flows into the sea. It's a good way to escape the crowds in high summer but you won't be alone – there is a beach bar and there is even a rough road from Ciutadella that goes most of the way to the beach (it is a 20-minute walk from the car park). Pine trees reach almost to the water's edge, providing welcome shade, and the beach shelves gently into the sea, creating good conditions for swimming. Many people consider this one of the most perfect spots on the Menorcan coast.

➕ 28B3
🍴 Cafeteria Susy (£)
🚌 Buses from Ferreries, Maó & Ciutadella to Cala Santa Galdana in summer
↔ Cala Santa Galdana (► 64)

Overlooking the bay on its western side are three large caves, once used as burial caves but now in service as holiday homes in summer. If you want more privacy, you can cross the headland above the caves to the even more perfect cove of Cala Macarelleta, where pine-fringed rocks surround a small sandy beach, popular with nudists. From the path on top of the headland you can look down on both coves at once, one of the best views anywhere on Menorca. The more adventurous can get between the two coves by swimming. Cala Macarella and Cala Macarelleta both offer good anchorage for yachts.

The footpath from Cala Santa Galdana to Cala Macarella and Cala Macarelleta (opposite)

61

29F2
Es Cap Roig (££)

CALA MESQUIDA ✪✪

Despite its proximity to Maó, this remains a peaceful and romantic spot. The capital's citizens come here at weekends, mainly to eat fish in the Cap Roig restaurant, on a slate headland carpeted with wild flowers. At the far end of the village is a wide beach of dark sand protected by cliffs to either side, one of which is dominated by an old watchtower. This was the site of the Duc de Crillon's landing with a Franco-Spanish invasion force in 1781. There is very little modern development (though this was one of Menorca's earliest beach resorts in the 19th century) and the village feels much more remote than it is – and more Menorcan than touristy.

28C3
None
Buses from Ferreries, Maó & Ciutadella to Cala Santa Galdana in summer
Cala Santa Galdana
(► 64)

Cala Mesquida is Maó's beach, where you see more locals than tourists

CALA MITJANA ✪✪

Situated down a small rocky track, this popular beach can be reached by car or on foot from Cala Santa Galdana (► 64). The walk starts in Camí de Cavalls above the eastern end of the bay – climb up the steps from the beach and turn left. At the end of this short road you go through a gate, bear left and continue through a gap in a wall; from here the way is clearly defined and marked with red dots. The walk takes about 30 minutes, passing the rocky cove of Cala Mitjaneta before arriving at a deep sandy beach surrounded by cliffs riddled with caves. The more adventurous can swim into some of the caves or leap from the cliffs into the cool blue water. The conditions here are also good for snorkelling.

CALA MORELL ✪✪

Eight kilometres from Ciutadella on the otherwise deserted northeast coast, Cala Morell is best known for its remarkable collection of prehistoric caves. Dating from the late Bronze and early Iron Ages, and used both as burial caves and as dwellings, they feature circular chambers with central pillars plus windows, chimneys and raised sleeping areas. Some even have elaborately carved motifs on their façades. It is easy to get into most of the caves; if your appetite is whetted, finds from these caves are on display at the Museu de Menorca in Maó (➤ 36) and the Museu Municipal in Ciutadella (➤ 41).

There is a small beach here, reached by steps from the car parks at either end of the village, and there is good swimming and snorkelling from the rock platforms at the foot of the cliffs. The *urbanización* above the beach, a collection of Ibizan-style whitewashed villas, is one of the most exclusive in Menorca. As you wander around the prehistoric caves, you cannot help wondering whether the tourists of 3,000 years' time will be clambering over the ruins of these villas and speculating on late 20th-century life.

➕ 28B4
🍴 Bars & restaurants (££)
↔ Cala d'Algaiarens (➤ 56)

CALA PREGONDA (➤ 17, TOP TEN)

CALA PRESILI ✪

A short walk from the headland at Cap de Favàritx (➤ 69) brings you to several quiet coves, beginning with Cala Presili. You start the walk by passing through wooden gates between a pair of white pillars 1km from the lighthouse. Cala Presili leads on to Cala Tortuga and then to Cala Morella Nou. All have high grassy dunes, clear white sand and good swimming – and none of them ever gets crowded. Behind the beach at Cala Tortuga is a marshy lake, part of the S'Albufera nature reserve (➤ 24).

➕ 29E3
🍴 None
↔ Cap de Favaritx (➤ 69)

Above: *Cala Morell, where you can play at being a caveman*

63

CALA SANTA GALDANA   ✪✪✪

One of Menorca's most beautiful (and ecologically important) coves is also one of the most developed – as such it has become a focus for debate about the extent of *urbanización* on the island. Thirty years ago there was not even a road here; now there are three enormous hotels and dozens of restaurants and bars.

The 'queen of the coves' takes its name from the Arab word for the local river; there is in fact no saint Galdana. A wide arc of golden sand, bounded by wooded cliffs and an emerald sea, Cala Santa Galdana enjoys a unique microclimate with higher temperatures and lower winds than the surrounding *calas*. The Barranc d'Algendar (➤ 16) flows into the sea here, its mouth widened to form a marina for small boats. A footbridge across the stream leads to a rocky outcrop, almost an island, and a spectacularly sited bar-restaurant where you dine on a terrace directly overlooking the sea. For the best views of the entire bay, follow the signs to Mirador de Sa Punta on the eastern cliffs, close to the start of the walk to Cala Mitjana (➤ 62). You can also climb up here from the steps at the eastern end of the beach.

This is a good place to go in mid-season as a base for walks along the gorge or to some of the quieter

beaches in both directions along the coast. In high season it is perfect for family holidays – fun and facilities for the children, safe swimming, and good shady walks for the adults. You can hire windsurfing and snorkelling equipment, pedaloes and motorboats, learn to sail or scuba-dive, or take a boat ride along the coast for a picnic at a peaceful cove.

Left and below left: *Cala Santa Galdana is a popular holiday destination, combining excellent facilities and an idyllic setting*

Did you know ?

Cala Santandría was the site of the French landing on Menorca on Easter Sunday 1756. Twelve thousand soldiers, commanded by the Duc de Richelieu, occupied Ciutadella without resistance as the British retreated to Maó. Richelieu sent the British Governor Blakeney a gift of dried fruits; Blakeney responded with six bottles of English beer. A month later Menorca was in French hands.

CALA SANTANDRÍA
This long, narrow creek, just 3km south of Ciutadella, would be pretty if it did not get so crowded. Along with its satellite cove Sa Caleta, it is the beach which Ciutadellans head for at weekends. There are several bars and restaurants, and all the usual facilities, including hire of pedal boats, umbrellas and loungers.

28A3
Bars & restaurants (£–££)
Buses from Ciutadella in summer
Cala Blanca (➤ 53)

CALA TIRANT
This pair of beaches between Fornells and Cap de Cavallería is reached either by taking the sign to 'Platges de Fornells' just outside Fornells and driving through the Menorca Country Club, or by following the dusty track 2km along the road to Cavallería which leads to the main beach. Both beaches are backed by dunes, marshland and a lake that attracts wading birds. The larger beach has a bar where you can hire umbrellas and sunbeds; there are also facilities for windsurfing and catamaran sailing. Swimming is safe and this is a good beach for children.

29D4
Beach bar/restaurant in summer (££)

CALA TREBALÚGER
This classic south coast cove, fed by a freshwater stream from a limestone gorge, is one of the hardest to reach. A popular mooring for yachts and pleasure boats in summer, it can only be reached on foot by a walk of about 1½ hours from Cala Santa Galdana (➤ 64) followed by a scramble down to the beach.

28C3
None
Boat trips from Cala En Bosc & Cala Santa Galdana in summer
Cala Mitjana (➤ 62)

In the Know

If you only have a short time to visit Menorca, or would like to get a real flavour of the island, here are some ideas:

Join the locals for a game of bowls in Maó's Plaça de S'Esplanada

10
Ways To Be A Local

Try to learn a little of the local language, Menorquín as well as Spanish – a simple *bon dia* goes a long way.

Relax, take your time and settle into the Mediterranean way of life.

Take a *siesta* to avoid the afternoon sun – have a long lunch, or rest in the shade.

Do everything late – a late lunch, a late supper, a very late night.

Put on your best clothes and join the evening *passeig*.

Go to the trotting races in Maó and Ciutadella at weekends – and be sure to have a bet.

Find a local *festa* – the best is the Festa de Sant Joan in Ciutadella – and let yourself get swept along by the crowd.

Go topless on the beach if you like but definitely not in restaurants and shops.

Respect the local environment – don't pick wild flowers or leave litter on the beaches.

Adore children – the Menorcans do.

10
Places To Have Lunch By The Sea

Ca'n Delio (££), ✉ Cales Fonts 38, Es Castell ☎ 971 35 17 11. Grilled sardines by a pretty harbour.

El Mirador (££), ✉ Cala Santa Galdana ☎ 971 15 45 03. The perfect setting on a terrace overlooking the sea.

Es Cap Roig (££), ✉ Cala Mesquida ☎ 971 18 83 83. Fresh fish and sea views on a headland north of Maó. Popular with locals.

Es Moll (££), ✉ Moll Commercial, Ciutadella ☎ 971 48 08 13. Watch the fishermen unload their catch while you eat.

Es Pla (£££), ✉ Fornells ☎ 971 37 66 55. Where the king comes to eat *caldereta de langosta*.

Gregal (££), ✉ Moll de Llevant 306, Maó ☎ 971 36 66 06. Modern Mediterranean dishes served beside the harbour at Cala Fiquera.

The Menorcans know the value of taking life at a steady pace

Il Girasole (££), Cala Blanca ☎ 971 38 51 68. Family restaurant with mini-golf and a toboggan slope to help keep the children amused while you eat Italian food.
Los Bucaneros (££), ✉ Platja de Binibèquer (No telephone). Simple restaurant in a wooden shack right on the beach. Seasonal only.
Susy (£), ✉ Cala Macarella ☎ 971 35 94 67. Summer bar and restaurant on one of Menorca's most beautiful beaches.

Tamarindos (££), ✉ Es Grau ☎ 971 35 94 20. Fresh fish and harbourside views with tables on a wooden jetty by the water's edge.

10
Top Activities

- Bird-watching
- Caving
- Diving
- Golf
- Horse-riding
- Sailing
- Swimming
- Walking
- Water-skiing
- Windsurfing

5
Family Beaches

- Arenal d'en Castell
- Cala Blanca
- Cala En Porter
- Cala Santa Galdana
- Son Parc

10
Best Viewpoints

- Cala Macarella/Cala Macarelleta – the headland
- Cap de Cavallería
- Cap de Favàritx
- Castell de Sant Nicolau, Ciutadella (at sunset)
- Cova d'en Xoroi, Cala En Porter
- Mirador de Sa Punta, Cala Santa Galdana
- Monte Toro
- Plaça de la Miranda, Maó
- Santa Águeda
- Son Mercer de Baix, Ferreries

5
Quiet Coves

- Cala del Pilar
- Cala En Turqueta
- Cala Escorxada
- Cala Macarelleta
- Cala Pudent (Son Parc)

The trotting races held in Maó and Ciutadella make a popular day out with both locals and tourists

✚ 29D2
🍴 None
🚌 Buses from Maó & Cala
En Porter to Son Vitamina
in summer

CALES COVES ★★★

It takes an effort to get there – a rough four-wheel-drive track or a brisk 30-minute walk through the olive trees from Son Vitamina – but when you arrive at Cales Coves you are greeted by one of the most memorable sights on Menorca. The cliffs looking down on to this sheltered bay are home to more than 100 Bronze Age caves, carved out of the rock and used as both burial chambers and dwellings, with the living and the dead housed side by side. The oldest caves, seen on the left as you arrive, date back to the 9th century BC; follow the footpath over the rocks on your right to reach a second cove, passing more modern caves (4th century BC) whose features include windows, patios and interior cubicles. Some of these have Roman inscriptions, indicating that they continued to be occupied after the Talaiotic period. Some of them, in fact, are still occupied by latter-day troglodytes; you see them collecting water from a spring and bathing nude in the crystal sea. From time to time the authorities try to move these modern cavemen on, but they always return. Peer into some of the uninhabited caves to see hippy paintings of suns, moons and flowers on the walls.

Carvings in the rock face at Cales Coves (top)

The prehistoric villagers chose a good site – the angle of the coves means they are hidden from the open sea. This also provides safe mooring for pleasure boats in summer. The beaches are pebbly rather than sandy, but there is good swimming from the rocks.

CAP DE CAVALLERÍA ✪✪

This headland at Menorca's northernmost point is one of the island's wild places. To get there you have to follow a potholed road across several kilometres of rocky moors, populated by wild goats. On the way you pass the tiny harbour of Sanitja. In Roman times this was the port of Sanisera, Menorca's third city. The results of recent excavations can be seen at **Ecomuseu Cap de Cavallería**, on the estate of Santa Teresa close to an old Roman settlement. Crossing cattle grids and passing through farm gates, eventually you reach the lighthouse at the end of the cape. Access to the lighthouse is barred but you can explore the headland on foot – if you can stand up in the wind. As you drive back towards civilisation, the hills around Monte Toro loom up like a much larger range of mountains than they actually are.

➕ 29D5
🍴 None

Ecomuseu Cap de Cavallería
☎ 971 35 99 99
🕐 Apr–Oct: daily 10–7
💷 Inexpensive

CAP DE FAVÀRITX ✪✪

Stand on Menorca's northeastern tip when the *tramuntana* is blowing and you will appreciate the island's savage beauty. Waves crash against crumbling slate cliffs, throwing sea-spray high into the air, and the solitary lighthouse acts as a reassuring reminder of humanity. The road from Maó is wide at first but eventually deteriorates into a bumpy track which in the end is little more than a causeway across the beach. From the cliffs at the end of the road you look out into an endless Mediterranean Sea. There are several quiet beaches which can be easily reached on foot from here, beginning with Cala Presili (➤ 63).

➕ 29F4
🍴 None
🔁 Cala Presili (➤ 63)

A wild goat at Cap de Cavallería: they get used to being photographed

ERMITA DE SANT JOAN DE MISSA ✪

This 15th-century Gothic church, brilliantly whitewashed and visible for miles around, is only used once a year – on the eve of the Festa de Sant Joan (➤ 116), when a horseback procession from Ciutadella rides out for a traditional Mass before returning to the city for the festivities. At most other times the church is locked, but if you're on your way to Cala En Turqueta (➤ 59) or Cala Macarella (➤ 61) it's worth stopping to look at the small gabled bell-tower and the ivy branches across the arched façade.

The Georgian town hall in the main square of Es Castell

ES CASTELL ✪✪

Founded by the British during their second occupation, and originally named Georgetown after George III, Es Castell retains the feel of a British colonial town. The Spanish renamed it Villacarlos after their own king; locals call it Es Castell because of its proximity to Fort Sant Felip (➤ 76). The main square, Plaça de S'Esplanada, is the former British parade ground, lined with solid Georgian buildings with sash windows and fanlights. Opposite the plum-red town hall, with its British clock tower, is the **Military Museum**, based in the old Cala Corb barracks. It contains a good collection of flags, guns and maps as well as model reconstructions of Fort Sant Felip and some fine 18th-century English furniture.

Es Castell is the most easterly town in Spain and thus the first to get the morning sun. Cales Fonts, a short walk from the main square, is an attractive sheltered harbour where you can dine at one of the many waterfront restaurants or pick up a boat tour of the Port de Maó (➤ 23).

A Walk From Es Castell

Start in Plaça de S'Esplanada, from outside the town hall.

Facing the military museum (➤ 70), head right along Carrer Cales Fonts. Go down into the small harbour of Cala Corb then up the other side to join Carrer Sant Cristòfol. At the end of this road turn left. Cross the roundabout and walk uphill. Turn left at the crossroads; just after passing Carrer des Fusters on the left, the road bends right.

Turn left at the entrance to the *depuradora* (water treatment plant) on a country lane that passes a large house and continues across farmland between walls, eventually reaching a road.

Cross the road and take the track opposite; when this joins another road bear right. Passing a military base, turn left on to a wide track marked Horts de Binissaida. At the end of this track, go left on a walled path – when the wall on your right runs out, climb through a gap and follow the footpath towards the sea.

Soon you drop down to Cala de Sant Esteve (p56), arriving beside the entrance to Fort Marlborough.

Walk around the bay and climb the narrow path at the far end to rejoin the road. Turn right at the cemetery. This road skirts the Sol del Este estate before reaching a small cove. Drop down to the beach then climb up the other side; continue through a modern estate and over another road. Turn right at the T-junction to reach Cales Fonts for lunch; from here, Carrer Stuart leads back to the main square.

Distance
10km

Time
2½ hours plus lunch

Start/end point
Es Castell
✚ 29F2
🚌 Bus from Maó

Lunch
Ca'n Delio (££)
✉ Cales Fonts 38
☎ 971 35 17 11

The harbour at Cales Fonts is perfectly placed to catch the midday sun

29D3
Bars & restaurants (££)
Buses from Maó & Ciutadella
Monte Toro (➤ 20)
Festa de Sant Martí third Sun in Jul

ES MERCADAL ✪✪

The name of this town gives away its origins – it was founded in the 14th century as a central market halfway between the ports of Maó and Ciutadella. Much later it was the setting for a defining moment in Menorcan history, when a meeting of his supporters in 1706 declared the Austrian archduke Charles, pretender to the Spanish throne, to be king – providing the pretext for the subsequent British invasion and occupation.

Nowadays Es Mercadal is a quiet town of plain white houses in the shadow of Menorca's highest mountain, Monte Toro (➤ 20). The main industries are the manufacture of *abarcas*, local sandals with soles made from recycled tyres, and the almond biscuits known as *amargas* and *carquinyols*.

This is the sort of sleepy place that tourism has passed by. Carrer Major, the old main street, is a long pedestrian thoroughfare which climbs gently from the central square past white-walled, green-shuttered houses. At the top of Carrer Major is an old windmill, one of several restaurants in the town specialising in traditional Menorcan cuisine.

Above: *Carrer Major in Es Mercadal – the house with the flags flying is the town hall*

ES MIGJORN GRAN ✪✪

The name of this quiet village means 'the large town in the south', *es migjorn* being the local term for the low limestone plateau, broken by gorges, which dominates the landscape of southern Menorca. For 200 years the village was known as San Cristóbal, after a blacksmith who founded a township here in 1769 – but before that it was known locally as Es Migjorn Gran and it has recently reverted to its old name.

This is the only one of the inland towns not on the Maó–Ciutadella highway and it retains a certain provincial charm. The main street, Carrer Major, is like a painting of old Menorca – simple white houses with balconies and green shutters, the few houses in bright blues and yellows providing an attractive contrast. During the *siesta* this street is deserted; then at 5PM it suddenly comes to life as ordinary-looking houses turn into shops and bars.

COVA DES COLOMS ✪✪

An easy excursion can be made from Es Migjorn Gran to this remarkable cave in the Binigaus gorge. Follow the signs from the Sant Tomàs end of the town. From the car park, walk past the cemetery and along a wide track to the farm of Binigaus Vell, then look for a track on your left (marked *cuevas*). Clamber over the wall to your left at another *cuevas* sign and follow the white arrows on the ground, crossing the valley floor to reach the cave. It is dank, dark, the size of a cathedral and buzzing with birds and bats. The cave can also be reached on foot from the beach at Sant Adeodato (► 82).

✚	28C3
🍴	Bars & restaurants (£–££)
🚌	Buses from Maó & Ferreries, & a link to Sant Tomàs in summer
↔	Sant Agustí Vell (► 82)
❓	Market Wed; Festa de Sant Cristòfol late Jul/early Aug

The parish church of Sant Cristòfol in Es Migjorn Gran

🏁 28C3
🍴 Lots of restaurants & bars (£–££)
🚌 Buses from Maó & Ciutadella
↔️ Binisues (➤ 52)
❓ Market Tue & Fri; farmers' and craft market Sat; Festa de Sant Bartomeu 23–25 Aug

Museu de la Natura
✉️ Carres Mallorca 2
☎️ 971 37 45 05
🕐 Tue–Sun 10–1, 6–9
👤 Inexpensive

Ferreries has few obvious sights, but that is part of its appeal

FERRERIES ⭐⭐

The highest town in Menorca – 150m above sea-level – was built in the shadow of the island's second-highest mountain, S'Enclusa. The name of the mountain means 'anvil' and it is thought the town's name derives from the word for 'blacksmith' – this was probably a centre of smithing along the road from Maó to Ciutadella. The main industries today are furniture and shoe manufacture; there are factory shops on the main road selling leather shoes.

Plaça d'Espanya, at the heart of the town, is a large modern square with a fountain and a children's play area. This is the venue for the popular farmers' market, with produce and craft stalls and folk-dancing displays. East and south of here are the wide avenues of the new town, which has expanded greatly since the 1940s; west and north are the narrow streets of a typical Menorcan town, all white houses with green shutters and a 19th-century parish church. Less pretty than its neighbours Es Mercadal and Es Migjorn Gran, Ferreries nevertheless retains an honest, lived-in feel – perhaps because the successful local industries mean that it is well-populated throughout the year. It is also developing a reputation as a centre for rural tourism; the **Museu de la Natura**, which opened in 1998, has exhibitions on environmental themes.

Just outside Ferreries is Son Mercer de Baix, an early Talaiotic village overlooking the confluence of two gorges (see opposite).

FORNELLS (➤ 18, TOP TEN)

A Walk Near Ferreries

This walk takes you deep into a valley for a close-up look at one of Menorca's limestone gorges. It is strenuous but spectacular, and easy to follow.

Start at the farm of Son Mercer de Dalt, 2km from Ferreries and reached by a wide track that begins 0.5km beyond the bridge on the road to Es Migjorn Gran. Take the track between the farmhouse drive and some barns, signposted Poblat de Son Mercer de Baix. After a few minutes, turn left on to a wide track; this passes through two gates then descends to the valley floor where you enter a lush field.

After five minutes you reach a secluded house. Cross the yard of the house, remembering to shut the gate, and continue on a lane above an orchard. When the lane divides, fork right to climb out of the valley. Climb for 20–30 minutes, then

go through a gate; a right turn at the next gate leads into a field and soon you see the farm of Son Mercer de Baix ahead. When you reach a junction with the farm on your right, turn left.

View from the top – looking down from Son Mercer de Baix

The next section is an optional extra but well worth it. An easy walk of around 1km brings you out at the prehistoric village of Son Mercer, where you can picnic among the *talaiots* and look down over the valley to see how far you have climbed.

Return along the same track but continue straight ahead through the farmyard. In the distance you see the impressive farmhouse of Son Mercer de Dalt – your destination.

Distance
8km

Time
2½ hours

Start/end point
Son Mercer de Dalt
 28C3
Bus to Ferreries then walk for 2km

Lunch
Take a picnic

75

♦ 29F2

🍴 None

↔ Port de Maó (➤ 23), Cala
de Sant Esteve (➤ 56),
Es Castell (➤ 70)

❓ Check local newspapers
or ☎ 971 36 21 00 for
details of guided tours

Above: *looking out from
Fort Sant Felip towards
the headland of La Mola*

Right: *Na Macaret, seen
from across the bay*

FORT SANT FELIP ✪✪

Not much remains of this once impregnable fortress,
begun at the southern entrance to Maó harbour following
the Turkish raids in the 16th century. It was the British
who strengthened it in the 18th century, using the most
modern military engineering techniques to create a
network of tunnels that allowed a whole garrison of
soldiers to live underground, out of sight of sea-borne
invaders. It was here that the British were holed up during

the French conquest of 1756; the 83-year-old General Blakeney only surrendered when it became clear that no help would arrive by sea. When the Spanish regained Menorca following the next period of British rule, one of their first acts was to destroy the fort. Whatever the reason, it was a disastrous mistake; the British were able to retake the island in 1798 without the loss of a single life. The fort now belongs to the Military Museum in Es Castell (► 70) and there are occasional guided tours. There are also regular tours of Fortaleza de la Mola, a 19th-century fortress on the opposite side of the harbour built out of the stone from Fort Sant Felip.

MONTE TORO (► 20, TOP TEN)

NA MACARET ✪

This old-fashioned seaside village 10km north of Alaior was one of the first Menorcan beach resorts in the 19th century – hence it avoided much of the vulgarity of the resorts that were developed much later. Rows of two-storey waterfront cottages face on to a small, sandy beach and a long narrow inlet which provides a perfect haven for yachts. There has been some recent development but it is relatively restrained.

29E4

Two restaurants by the beach (££)

Arenal d'en Castell (► 49), Port d'Addaia (► 78)

NAVETA DES TUDONS (➤ 21, TOP TEN)

PORT D'ADDAIA   ✪

Menorca's third-longest natural harbour, more than 3km long and 400m wide, is popular with the yachting set because of the protection it provides from the *tramuntana* wind. John Armstrong, who wrote the first English guide to Menorca in 1752, described this as the most perfect place on the island, and it is certainly very attractive. From the marina you look out across the masts of the yachts to a long, woody inlet and a sea framed by cliffs and small islands. This was the site of the final British invasion of Menorca in 1798, when Britain managed to capture the island without loss of life following the destruction of Fort Sant Felip by the Spanish. Inevitably a resort has mushroomed above the marina but the waterside itself remains blissfully unspoilt.

PUNTA NATI   ✪

Drive out here on a windy day – or better still, take a bike – and you will see why Menorca is called an island of stones and wind. The 6km road to the island's northwestern tip has little to offer apart from endless vistas of a barren, rocky landscape punctuated by stepped *ponts*, the drystone sheep and cattle sheds which protect the livestock from the extremes of the weather and help clear the fields of unwanted stones. On the wind-buffeted headland, as ever, the lighthouse is off limits, but you can walk along the cliffs to a couple of deserted coves.

The attractive marina at Port d'Addaia

PUNTA PRIMA

The southeastern extremity of Menorca boasts one of the island's largest and finest beaches – but the currents in this part of Menorca can be dangerous and swimmers should pay particular attention to the Red Cross flag and only swim if the green flag is flying.

This is a popular area for watersports – you can hire windsurfing and sailing equipment, as well as pedal boats, on the beach. Facing Punta Prima across the sea is the Illa de l'Aire, an uninhabited island with an automatic lighthouse, clear sea-beds for diving and a small harbour for yachts. The island is the home of a rare species of black lizard.

29F1
Restaurants & bars
(£–££)
Buses from Maó & Sant Lluís in summer and a road train from Binibeca Vell in summer

Above: *timeless pleasures on the beach at Punta Prima*

RAFAL RUBÍ NOU

Most people head for the Naveta des Tudons (➤ 21) to see the best-preserved example of a burial *naveta*; but it can be just as exciting to discover the lesser Bronze Age sites away from the beaten path. Signposted down a country lane on the main highway 6.7km west of Maó, Rafal Rubí consists of two *navetas* set in the middle of farmland.

29E2
Free access
None
Talatí de Dalt (➤ 88)

S'ABUFERA DES GRAU (➤ 24, TOP TEN)

Did you know ?

When the British governor was under siege from the French in Fort Sant Felip in 1756, a fleet of ships under Admiral Byng sailed from Gibraltar to protect him. They reached the Illa de l'Aire and were all set to proceed on Maó harbour; but they turned and fled back to Gibraltar instead. The British surrendered; Byng was court-martialled and shot 'to encourage the others', as Voltaire put it.

28B4

✉ 2km from Ciutadella on Camí Vell de Maó

☎ 971 48 15 78

🕐 Daily 9:30–1:30, 5–9 in summer; free access in winter

🍴 None

↔ Ciutadella (► 38), Torre Trencada (► 90)

Above: *the quarry at S'Hostal near Ciutadella*

S'HOSTAL ⭐⭐

Menorca's most unusual tourist attraction is a disused sandstone quarry outside Ciutadella, which has been turned into a monument to the island's history and traditions of quarrying. Sandstone has been used for building since prehistoric times; soft and permeable, hence easy to extract, it turns hard when exposed to the air and is the perfect building material. Traditionally it was extracted by hammer and chisel; the few remaining quarries use circular saws which dig deep into the ground, creating vertical walls of white stone.

The quarry closed in 1994; it was bought up by Líthica and reopened the following year. You can walk around a 'labyrinth of orchards' in the old quarry, now being turned into a garden, then descend to the giant white amphitheatre of the modern quarry, 30m deep, where on weekdays workmen give displays of quarrying and at other times you stand in the eerie quiet of a sandstone cathedral. Líthica has ambitious plans for this site – a maze, a sculpture park, a visitor centre, a concert auditorium beneath the sheer white walls. An industrial wasteland has been creatively transformed into an unexpectedly special place.

29E3

🕐 Free access

🍴 None

↔ S'Albufera des Grau (► 24)

SA TORRETA ⭐

One of the few Talaiotic sites in northern Menorca is also one of the hardest to reach; the best way is the walk from Es Grau (► facing page). Overgrown and evocative, a complete *taula* 4m high is surrounded by standing stones on the edge of a farm. Tests show that this was built 1,000 years after the *taulas* at Son Catlar (► 86) and Trepucó (► 90) – so the Talaiotic culture was certainly not short-lived.

A Coastal Walk to Sa Torreta

This walk has everything – countryside, archaeology, beaches and coastal views.

Begin at Es Grau (➤ 24), walking around the beach to the far side opposite the car park. Climb the footpath on to the cliffs and turn right. Ignore all junctions and continue until you see Illa d'en Colom ahead. Follow the path down towards the sea, passing a cave house and crossing behind a small beach.

The path now swings left to cross a headland and drops to Fondeadero de los Llanes.

Walk around this bay, passing two inlets and a sandy beach, then up a slope on the far side. Climb over the wall to reach a sandy area and look for a narrow gap on the left leading to the cart-track. Note this spot carefully – there is a red arrow on a stone to guide you – and turn left.

An easy circular walk returns you to this spot. The track skirts the S'Albufera lagoon then climbs to Sa Torreta farm after 30–40 minutes.

At the farm, an overgrown path beside a concrete barn leads to Sa Torreta (➤ facing page). Leaving the farm, take the track straight ahead. The track descends to Cala de Sa Torreta, shaded by pine woods, then climbs above the bay, passing another beach before turning inland. Now look for the junction where you began the circular walk. Turn left to return to Es Grau by the same route.

At Es Grau beach, go through the gap between the dunes to cross part of the S'Albufera reserve. You emerge on the main road a few minutes south of the village.

Distance
11km

Time
3 hours plus picnic

Start/end point
Es Grau
✚ 29F3
🚌 Buses from Maó in summer

Lunch
Take a picnic

The walk from Es Grau leads along a wild section of the coast

28C2

🍴 Beach bar in summer; restaurants at Sant Tomàs (££)

🚌 Buses to Sant Tomàs from Maó, Ciutadella & Es Migjorn Gran in summer

↔ Sant Tomàs (➤ 84)

SANT ADEODATO ✪

The western end of Sant Tomàs beach (➤ 84), beyond the road from Es Migjorn Gran, is totally undeveloped and known as Sant Adeodato. The sand is fine, the swimming is safe but there are few beach facilities. A short walk on a sandy path behind the beach, passing the islet of Binicodrell offshore, brings you to the larger beach at Binigaus, popular with nudists but with dangerous currents that make it unsafe for swimming. From Binigaus you can walk inland along the Barranc de Binigaus, a limestone gorge riddled with caves, including the cathedral-like Cova des Coloms – though the easier approach to this particular cave is from Es Migjorn Gran (➤ 73).

28C3

⊙ Free access

🍴 None

🚌 Buses to Es Migjorn Gran from Maó & Ferreries

↔ Es Migjorn Gran (➤ 73)

Above: the quiet beach at Sant Adeodato is dwarfed by its neighbour, Sant Tomàs

SANT AGUSTÍ VELL ✪

This is one of the hardest of Menorca's prehistoric sites to find but that makes the effort all the more rewarding and you will probably be alone with your thoughts when you get there. Take the road from Es Migjorn Gran to Sant Tomàs; after 1km, an unsigned track to your right leads to the farm of Sant Agustí. Park just off the main road and walk along this track. At the farm gates, go right, through a gate marked *cuevas*; when you see a pair of litter bins you know that you have reached the site. The main attraction here is a large *talaiot* with a beamed roof of olive and juniper wood; once they would all have been like this but this is the only one that survives. The village was strategically situated at the head of the Binigaus gorge, and the *cuevas* referred to include the Cova d'en Coloms.

SANT CLIMENT ★

Unusually for the Mediterranean, this is a self-contained community where many locals grew up in the village and have lived there ever since – though most now work in Maó or at the airport, just a Balearic slingshot away. The village has two bars, a chemist, a baker, a newsagent and a mini-market, plus the inevitable main square with palm trees at its corners and an 18th-century church with a 20th-century façade.

✚ 29E2
🍴 Bars (£) & Casino San Clemente (££)
🚌 Buses from Maó
↔ Torelló (► 88)
❓ Festa de Sant Climent – third weekend in Aug

SANT LLUÍS ★★

Even by Menorcan standards, Sant Lluís is white – when the sun is shining, it fairly sparkles. Founded by the French in 1761 during their brief occupation of Menorca to provide housing for their troops, it is laid out in a grid style around a series of attractive squares. The town was named after Louis IX, to whom the huge, whitewashed, buttressed church is dedicated; the west front contains the coats of arms of the French royal family as well as the Comte de Lannion, Menorca's first French governor.

A blue and white windmill, **Molí de Dalt**, seen as you enter the town from Maó, has been turned into a small folk museum with a collection of old farm implements – the main square opposite the windmill contains a good children's playground. Despite having become virtually a suburb of Maó, Sant Lluís remains a quiet, pretty town with a laid-back atmosphere and, perhaps surprisingly given its origins, a large British community. The hamlet of Torret to the south contains some of the finest traditional rural houses on the island.

✚ 29E2
🍴 Restaurants & bars (££)
🚌 Buses from Maó
❓ Festa de Sant Lluís – last weekend in Aug
Molí de Dalt
☎ 971 15 10 84
💲 Inexpensive

The Molí de Dalt windmill announces your arrival in Sant Lluís

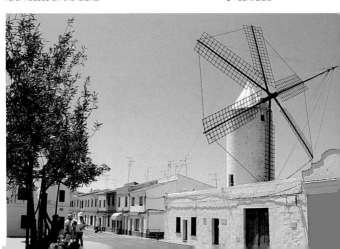

28C2

🍴 Restaurants & bars (££)

🚌 Buses from Maó, Ciutadella & Es Migjorn Gran in summer

↔ Sant Adeodato (➤ 82)

SANT TOMÀS ✪

This long beach of pale golden sand is virtually a continuation of the beach at Son Bou (➤ 25), separated from it by a pair of low headlands. Once a quiet spot, it has grown into a major resort with four large hotels and an *urbanización* creeping up the hills behind the beach. In 1989 a freak storm blew away all the sand from the beach and what you see now has been imported in its place. A path at the western end of the beach leads to the quieter beaches of Sant Adeodato and Binigaus (➤ 82). Take note of the flag system for safe bathing as the beach has dangerous currents.

 28C4

🍴 None

↔ Binisues (➤ 52)

SANTA AGUEDA ✪✪

Climbing Menorca's third-highest hill today, there is little to suggest that it once supported the island's most significant fortress. Built by the Romans and strengthened by the Moors, the castle on Santa Agueda's summit was the last Muslim stronghold to resist the Catalan conquest in 1287.

The buildings have fallen into disrepair and only the serious archaeologist would recognise the Roman, Arab and Spanish influences – but it is still worth the walk up here for the views, which stretch to both Maó and Ciutadella and along the windswept north coast. As a bonus, the path to the summit takes you along the best-preserved Roman road in Menorca. To get there, take the Binisues road, signposted off the C721 3km west of Ferreries; after another 3km, park by an old white schoolhouse and go through the gate to begin your walk. The climb to the summit takes a brisk 20–30 minutes. This is a popular picnic spot, much used by local families at weekends.

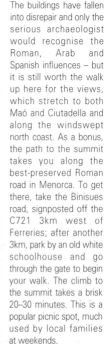

SHANGRI-LA (ALBUFERA) ✪

The name means 'an imaginary paradise', and imaginary it has turned out to be. Conceived in the tourist boom of the 1970s as an up-market golf resort on the shores of the S'Albufera lake (➤ 24), Shangri-La was the subject of years of legal and political argument before being finally halted on the grounds that it represented illegal development in a conservation area. By this time many of the houses had been built; some were already lived in. The victory for Menorca's environmental campaigners proved to be a landmark, as the island realised that tourism had to be controlled. But a half-built *urbanización* is even worse than a finished one, and if you wander around Shangri-La today you are bound to be struck by the air of desolation, with the golf course overgrown and villas abandoned when the money ran out. In a vain attempt to improve its image, the resort is now known as Albufera. It serves as a lesson to anyone else tempted to create a new 'village' and call it paradise.

🚑 29E3
🍴 None
🚌 Buses from Maó to Es Grau in summer
↔ S'Albufera d'es Grau (➤ 24)

Above: *life is non-stop fun at the Club San Jaime near Son Bou*

SO NA CAÇANA ✪

A short walk south of Torre Llisà Vell (➤ 90) on the Alaior to Cala En Porter road, this Bronze Age site with two *talaiots* and two *taulas* – both with their horizontal stone missing – is one of Menorca's least-visited archaeological sites. It is certainly not worth a detour, but if you have got out of your car already to see Torre Llisà Vell you may want to combine the two. Get there through a gap in the wall beside the main road.

🚑 29D2
⊘ Free access
🍴 None
↔ Torralba d'en Salord (➤ 89), Torre Llisà Vell (➤ 90)

Opposite: *a well-preserved Roman road leads to the summit of Santa Agueda*

SON BOU (➤ 25, TOP TEN)

Was it built by giants? The outer wall of Son Catlar

28B3
Free access
None
Arenal de Son Saura
(► 49)

SON CATLAR

Menorca's largest megalithic settlement is reached on the road from Ciutadella to Arenal de Son Saura. Built around 1800 BC, it grew to its present size in Roman times and continued to be occupied right up to the Middle Ages. The most impressive feature here is the surrounding wall, some 900m in circumference and built of massive stones – walls such as this one are often known as Cyclopean because of the belief that only giants could have built them. A doorway at the north side of the wall leads to a *taula* precinct, but the horizontal stone on top of the *taula* has fallen and collapsed. Unlike most prehistoric sites on Menorca, Son Catlar has helpful, multi-lingual information boards to guide you around.

29D4
Bars & restaurants
(£–££), including beach
bar in summer
Buses from Maó &
Fornells in summer

SON PARC

A dreary *urbanización*, with a golf course and hundreds of identical apartments, leads to this perfect beach, which is large enough not to get too crowded even in high summer. The water is shallow, there are pedaloes and motorboats for hire, and the dunes and pine woods at the back of the beach offer some relief from the sun. As so often in Menorca, there is also a peaceful cove just a short walk away from a busy resort. Take the path through a gap in the wall at the west end of the beach, walk for 20 minutes across the headland breathing in the pungent mix of wild rosemary and salty sea breeze, cross a shingle beach, climb a hillock and then drop to Cala Pudent where, out of season, you can have the beach to yourself.

A Drive Along the Camí d'en Kane

When the British moved the capital to Maó, they also built a new road from Maó to Ciutadella – financed by a tax on alcohol. Parts of the road, named after the first British governor, still exist and have been restored.

Start by the ferry station on the waterfront at Maó. Take the road north for Fornells. Shortly after leaving the harbour you pass a monument to Sir Richard Kane on your right. After another 2km, turn left on to a quiet country road, the Camí d'en Kane.

This road rises and falls through typical Menorcan countryside – meadows, cattle, drystone walls. After 9km you see the town of Alaior to your left and a cemetery on your right.

Keep straight ahead as the road narrows and passes beneath a canopy of pine trees.

Monte Toro rises up ahead of you – a recurring feature of the next few kilometres. Eventually Camí d'en Kane ends and you join the main highway from Maó to Ciutadella (from here it roughly follows the route of Kane's original road).

Turn right and almost immediately right again, skirting the town of Es Mercadal and following signs to Fornells.

Continue to this beautiful fishing village (➤ 18) for lunch by the harbour.

Leave Fornells by the same road; after 3km, turn left towards Maó.

This road passes through some of Menorca's most thickly wooded areas before returning to Maó harbour. Several roads to the left lead to various north coast resorts, including Arenal d'en Castell (➤ 49) and Son Parc (➤ facing page).

Distance
56km

Time
1½ hours plus lunch

Start point
Maó harbour
🚩 29F2

End point
Maó

Lunch
S'Ancora (££)
✉ Passeig Marítim 8, Fornells
☎ 971 37 66 70

View along the Camí d'en Kane

TALATÍ DE DALT ✪✪

🟦 29E2
✉ Signposted off the Maó–Ciutadella road, 4km from Maó
🎫 Free access
🍴 None
🔁 Rafal Rubí Nou (➤ 79), Torelló (see below)

Like many of Menorca's prehistoric monuments, Talatí de Dalt blends so well into its surroundings that it is difficult to tell which of the piles of stones are ancient and which modern. A wild olive tree grows inside the *taula* precinct; bushes sprout out of a *talaiot* and standing stones are scattered around a field. The central *taula* is one of the largest in Menorca; a separate pillar leans against it, probably a result of an accident. The site dates from 1400 BC, but it was inhabited until at least Roman times.

TORELLÓ ✪✪

🟦 29E2
✉ Off the Maó–Sant Climent road
🎫 Free access
🍴 None
🔁 Sant Climent (➤ 83), Talatí de Dalt (see above)

Two sites separated by 300m and a millennium of history are found in the shadow of a modern airport. The *talaiot* here, one of the largest in Menorca, is often the first that visitors see – it is visible from incoming planes.

Of more interest is the 6th-century basilica, Es Fornàs de Torelló, discovered in 1956 by a farmer ploughing up his fields. The church, built under Byzantine rule, is protected by a corrugated iron roof – but you can walk around the viewing platform and marvel at the motifs of peacocks, lions and palm trees on the mosaic floor. Parts of the altar survive, as does the baptismal font; the design suggests an African influence, indicating early links with the North African church.

Above: *an ancient chamber at Talatí de Dalt*

TORRALBA D'EN SALORD   ⊙⊙

This extensive site, 3km south of Alaior, is the closest Menorca has come to turning its prehistoric ruins into a tourist attraction. The road that used to bisect the site has been diverted, a car and coach park created, and arrows have been put up to guide visitors around Menorca's first archaeological park – the only ancient site in Menorca to levy an admission charge. There are the remains of a complete village here, including a *taula*, two *talaiots* and a Cyclopean wall, along with artificial burial caves. From the village there are good views of the white town of Alaior with Monte Toro (▶ 20) towering over it in the distance.

TORRE D'EN GAUMÉS (▶ 26, TOP TEN)

TORRE LLAFUDA   ⊙

This little-visited site off the highway from Maó to Ciutadella contains a complete *taula*, less than 2m tall and romantically surrounded by a halo of wild olive and holm oak. Near the *taula* are a set of burial caves and some well-preserved defensive walls. Among the finds here was a Roman gold ring engraved with the figure of a camel; like many prehistoric sites, Torre Llafuda continued to be occupied well into Roman times and possibly much later.

> ### *Did you know ?*
>
> *One of the objects found at Torralba d'en Salord was a bronze figure of a calf – suggesting that the bull was venerated in Menorca in ancient times as it was elsewhere in the Mediterranean. One of the many theories about taulas is that they may have been worshipped as stylised images of bulls.*

🚩 29D2
✉ On the Alaior–Cala En Porter road
🕐 Daily 10–8
🍴 Refreshment kiosk
💰 Inexpensive
🔁 Alaior (▶ 48), Torre Llisà Vell (▶ 90)

🚩 28B3
✉ Signposted off the Maó–Ciutadella road at 37km
🕐 Free access
🍴 None
🔁 Naveta des Tudons (▶ 21)

Above: *excavations at Torralba d'en Salord suggest that the site was used for ritual animal sacrifices*

TORRE LLISÀ VELL ✪

This is the sort of place that makes seeking out Menorca's ancient monuments worthwhile – even if you have no interest in archaeology. Turn right off the Alaior to Cala En Porter road 5km south of Alaior at the crossroads marked 'Camí de Cutaines'; park at the farm and follow red arrows through the fields to reach the *taula* precinct, enclosed by its original wall. A perfectly preserved stone archway, perhaps 3,000 years old, guards the precinct – as you stoop beneath the ancient arch you wonder just how many people have stood there before you and why.

TORRE TRENCADA ✪

Drive across farmland on the old Roman road from Ciutadella to Maó, turn into a small car park, cross three cattle grids and across a field you catch sight of a monumental *taula* hiding among the trees. Birds sing and cattle graze as you cross the field; the prehistoric village is surrounded by drystone walls and as with so many of Menorca's ancient sites it is hard to tell where the old stones end and the new ones begin.

TREPUCÓ ✪✪

On the outskirts of Maó are a massive *taula* and *talaiot*. which have stood for 3,000 years while invaders have come and gone. The *taula* here, 4m high, is the tallest in Menorca. The complex is surrounded by a star-shaped wall, built by the Duc de Crillon in 1782 when the French were laying siege to Fort Sant Felip (➤ 76) and used Trepucó as their base. In 1931 the site was excavated by Margaret Murray, who found small boys playing on top of the overgrown *taula*. A notice asks visitors not to climb on the ruins.

✚ 29D2
◎ Free access
🍴 None
↔ So Na Caçana (➤ 85), Torralba d'en Salord (➤ 89)

✚ 28B3
◎ Free access
🍴 None
↔ S'Hostal (➤ 80)

✚ 29F2
✉ Signposted off the Maó–Sant Lluis road
◎ Free access
🍴 None
↔ Maó (➤ 30)

The taula and talaiot at Trepucó

Where To...

Above: *chairs at Binimel-là*
Below: *children playing in Es Castell*

Maó

Prices

Prices are approximate, based on a three-course meal for one without drinks and service:

£ = under 12 euros
££ = 12–24 euros
£££ = over 24 euros

Most restaurants serve a *menú del día* (► 95) at lunchtime (and sometimes in the evening) which will usually work out much cheaper. It is normal practice to add about 10 per cent to the bill as a tip.

American Bar (£)

Busy meeting-place in the heart of the pedestrian shopping district.

✉ **Plaça Reial 8** ☎ **971 36 18 22** 🕐 **Closed weekend evenings**

Andaira (££–£££)

Creative Mediterranean cuisine in a town house with a lemon-shaded courtyard. The lunchtime set menu is excellent value.

✉ **Carrer des Forn 61** ☎ **971 36 68 17** 🕐 **Lunch & dinner. Closed Sun and Mon in winter**

Ca'n Nito (££)

Fresh fish and lobster near the foot of the harbour steps.

✉ **Moll de Llevant 15** ☎ **971 36 52 26** 🕐 **Lunch & dinner. Closed Sun in winter**

Casa Sexto (££)

Fishy *tapas* and seafood specialities – the owner flies in fresh seafood from his native Galicia and cooks it in sea water while you wait.

✉ **Carrer Vassallo 2** ☎ **971 36 84 07** 🕐 **Lunch & dinner. Closed Sun and Mon lunch**

El Viejo Almacen (££)

Trendy waterfront *tapas* bar specialising in barbecued meat and vegetables. Try the Basque-style *pintxos*, nibbles of bread topped with ham, anchovies or cheese.

✉ **Moll de Llevant 75** ☎ **971 36 89 52** 🕐 **Tue–Sun 12–12**

Es Fosquet (£££)

Intimate harbourside fish restaurant in an old cave with whitewashed walls and an outdoor terrace. Daily selection of fresh fish, which might include sea-bream, bass or Menorcan prawns.

✉ **Moll de Llevant 256** ☎ **971 35 00 58** 🕐 **Dinner only, May–Sep**

Gregal (££)

Locals consider this one of the best harbourside restaurants in Cala Figuera.

✉ **Moll de Llevant 306** ☎ **971 36 66 06** 🕐 **Lunch & dinner**

Il Porto (££)

Pizzas, barbecues and grilled vegetables in an open-plan setting on the waterfront.

✉ **Moll de Llevant 225** ☎ **971 35 44 26** 🕐 **Lunch & dinner (dinner only in Jul and Aug)**

Itake (££)

One of the few waterfront restaurants not to concentrate on fish. Fashionable and offbeat.

✉ **Moll de Llevant 317** ☎ **971 35 45 70** 🕐 **Lunch Tue–Sat, dinner Tue–Sun**

Jàgaro (£££)

Fresh seafood and views from the harbourside terrace are the attractions at this top-notch Cala Figuera restaurant.

✉ **Moll de Llevant 334** ☎ **971 36 23 90** 🕐 **Lunch & dinner**

L'Arpó (££)

Pretty waterfront bistro specialising in simple fresh fish and *paella*.

✉ **Moll de Llevant 124** ☎ **971 36 98 44** 🕐 **Lunch & dinner. Closed Wed lunch**

La Minerva (£££)

Upscale restaurant set in an old flour mill, with six different dining-rooms and a floating terrace. Mediterranean nouvelle cuisine as well as traditional lobster *paella*.

✉ **Moll de Llevant 87** ☎ **971 35 19 95** 🕐 **Lunch & dinner**

La Sirena (££)
German-run bistro serving *comida integral* (wholefood cooking), with a range of organic meat, fish and vegetarian dishes. Asian and Mediterranean influences.

✉ Moll de Llevant 199
☎ 971 35 07 40 ⏰ Dinner only. Closed Tue

La Tropical (££)
One of the few good restaurants in the city centre; includes a daily 'menu from the market'.

✉ Carrer La Lluna 36 ☎ 971 36 05 56 ⏰ Lunch & dinner. Closed Wed

Latitud 40° (££)
Late-night harbourside bar specialising in *tapas*, grilled vegetables and cheese.

✉ Moll de Llevant 265 ☎ 971 36 41 76 ⏰ Mon–Sat 4PM–3AM

Marès (£££)
Modern Mediterranean cuisine in a converted 18th-century palace. For a snack or drink, try the café terrace overlooking the port.

✉ Plaça de la Conquesta
☎ 971 36 95 76 ⏰ Lunch Tue–Sun, dinner Tue–Sat; café Mon–Sat 9AM–10PM

Marivent (£££)
Possibly the best of numerous harbourside restaurants in Cala Figuera; tables on the terrace look down over the port. Mainly fish and seafood but there are also exquisite grilled meat dishes.

✉ Moll de Llevant 314 ☎ 971 36 98 01 ⏰ Lunch and dinner. Closed Sun

Meson del Puerto (££)
Classic Basque seafood cuisine in a lively area beside the ferry port.

✉ Moll de Ponent 66 ☎ 971 35 29 03 ⏰ Closed Sun

Nashville (££)
The ultimate in cultural confusion – pizzas, German and Tex-Mex dishes in this 'beer and soundhouse' down by the sea.

✉ Moll de Llevant 145 ☎ 971 36 79 56 ⏰ Lunch & dinner

Roma (£)
Fashionable, reasonably priced pizzeria.

✉ Moll de Llevant 295 ☎ 971 35 37 77 ⏰ Lunch & dinner. Closed Thu lunch

S'Espigo (££)
Small, stylish restaurant with a wide range of fish baked in sea salt.

✉ Moll de Llevant 267 ☎ 971 36 99 09 ⏰ Closed Sun lunch

San José (££)
British-run farmhouse restaurant on the Fornells road. Book in advance.

✉ Carretera Maó–Fornells
☎ 971 35 17 59 ⏰ Apr–Oct: dinner Mon–Sat, Sun lunch

Taj (££)
Maó's Indian restaurant has a waterfall in its back garden, where children can play safely while you eat.

✉ Sinie d'es Muret 23 ☎ 971 35 40 70 ⏰ Apr–Oct: dinner only

Varadero (£££)
Swish, expensive harbourside restaurant offering designer *paellas* and fish dishes such as monkfish casserole and salmon in *cava*. Beside the jetty where cruise ships disembark.

✉ Moll de Llevant 4 ☎ 971 35 20 74 ⏰ Lunch & dinner. Closed Sun

Opening Times
The Spanish like to eat late – many restaurants do not even open until 1:30 at lunchtime and 8:30 in the evening, and fill up an hour or two later. Most restaurants either close down for the winter or severely reduce their opening times, so it is always a good idea to check in advance. *Tapas* bars tend to be open throughout the day.

Ciutadella

Tapas

Tapas are a Spanish institution. Originally a free 'lid' (*tapa*) of ham across a drink, nowadays they consist of small portions of everything from octopus to olives. Locals tend to eat *tapas* before going home for dinner, but several portions can make a filling meal in itself. And you don't have to look at a menu – just point to what you want in the cabinet.

Aurora (£)

Fishy *tapas* and fresh seafood on a lively square where the old town meets the new.

✉ **Plaça Alfons III 3** ☎ **971 38 00 29** 🍴 **Lunch & dinner**

Café Balear (££)

The perfect setting for lunch by the harbour; plenty of fresh shellfish plus steaks and *carpaccio* of veal.

✉ **Passeig de Sant Joan 17** ☎ **971 38 00 05** 🍴 **Lunch & dinner. Closed Sun in summer, Mon in winter**

Ca'n Nito (££)

Tapas bar on the edge of the Born with lots of fish dishes and charcoal-grilled steaks.

✉ **Plaça des Born 11** ☎ **971 48 07 68** 🍴 **All day**

Casa Manolo (£££)

Top-notch fresh seafood and lobster dishes beside the harbour walls.

✉ **Port de Ciutadella** ☎ **971 38 00 03** 🍴 **Lunch & dinner**

Chinatown Two (££)

The set menu at this Cantonese restaurant is one of the best bargains in town.

✉ **Carrer Mallorca 34** ☎ **971 48 08 71** 🍴 **Lunch & dinner**

Club Náutico (££)

Serious fish dishes in the yacht club restaurant overlooking the port.

✉ **Cami Baix, beneath Passeig Maritim** ☎ **971 38 27 73** 🍴 **Lunch & dinner**

Don Giacomo (££)

Italian-Mediterranean cuisine, such as wood-fired pizzas and Catalan-inspired meat dishes, served in a town house with vaulted ceilings and original stone walls.

✉ **Carrer Nou de Juliol 5** ☎ **971 38 32 79** 🍴 **Lunch & dinner, Tue–Sun**

El Bribón (££)

Down by the harbour it's a question of just taking your pick, but this seafood restaurant and *tapas* bar is better value than most.

✉ **Port de Ciutadella** ☎ **971 38 50 50** 🍴 **Lunch & dinner**

El Horno (££)

Intimate basement French restaurant near the Plaça des Born.

✉ **Carrer des Forn 12** ☎ **971 38 07 67** 🍴 **Dinner only, Apr–Oct**

Es Fabiol (£)

A branch of the Ses Voltes string of restaurant-bars in Ciutadella, specialising in pizzas, baguettes and Menorcan sausages. In summer you can eat outside on the shady square.

✉ **Plaça de S'Esplanada** ☎ **971 48 23 70** 🍴 **Lunch & dinner**

Es Lloc (£££)

This hotel restaurant has an excellent reputation for creative Menorcan and Mediterranean cuisine. Seasonal menu.

✉ **Hotel Sant Ignasi, Carretera de Cala Morell** ☎ **971 38 55 75** 🍴 **Lunch & dinner in summer, weekends only in winter**

Es Moll (££)

Some of the freshest fish you'll ever find in a beautiful setting beside the harbour. The lunchtime *menú del dia* is especially good value.

✉ **Moll Comercial** ☎ **971 48 08 13** 🍴 **Lunch & dinner**

La Guitarra (££)
Classic Menorcan dishes –
duck, roast lamb, snails – in
an atmospheric cellar.
✉ **Carrer Nostra Senyora dels
Dolors 1** ☎ **971 38 13 55**
🕒 **Closed Sun**

La Payesa (££)
A large choice of seafood
dishes including three
different *paellas*, plus a
children's menu.
✉ **Port of Ciutadella** ☎ **971
38 00 21** 🕒 **Lunch & dinner**

Oristano (£)
Fresh pasta and wood-fired
pizzas in an old shoe factory
overlooking the Pla de Sant
Joan. Popular with a late-
night crowd at weekends.
✉ **Carrer Borja Moll 1** ☎ **971
38 41 97** 🕒 **Dinner only**

Pa Amb Oli (££)
The name means 'bread and
oil', a popular local snack
served with platters of
sausages, ham, grilled
vegetables or grilled meat in
this busy restaurant close to
Plaça des Born.
✉ **Carrer Nou de Juliol 4**
☎ **971 38 36 19** 🕒 **Lunch &
dinner**

Racó des Palau (££)
Fish, pizzas and Italian
cuisine in the back streets
behind the Palau Salord.
✉ **Carrer des Palau 3** ☎ **971
38 54 02** 🕒 **Apr–Oct. Closed
Sun lunch**

Restaurant d'Es Port (££)
Fresh fish, seafood and
grilled meats with a view of
the fishing port. The main
restaurant features lobster
and fish from their own
fishing boat, while the more
informal brasserie has pizzas
and a children's menu.
✉ **Port de Ciutadella** ☎ **971
48 00 22** 🕒 **Lunch & dinner**

Roma (££)
Part of the Café Balear chain,
the speciality here is pizzas
cooked in a wood-fired oven.
Also Italian meat and fish
dishes and fresh pasta.
✉ **Carrer Pere d'Alcántara 18**
☎ **971 38 47 18** 🕒 **Closed
Sun lunch**

Sa Figuera (£££)
Grilled steaks and seafood
dishes, including *caldereta
de langosta*.
✉ **Port de Ciutadella** ☎ **971
38 21 12** 🕒 **Lunch & dinner**

Sa Gelateria de Menorca (£)
The best ice cream in
Menorca. Flavours include
almond, cinnamon and fig, as
well as a refreshing
granizado de limón (lemon
slush).
✉ **Plaça de la Catedral 3 and
Costa des Port 69** ☎ **971 38 11
92** 🕒 **Daily 10AM–2AM in
summer**

Sa Llesca (££)
Good for lunchtime snacks
beneath the parasols on a
lively old town square. Try the
llesca – toast rubbed with
tomato and topped with
anchovies, ham, Menorcan
sausages or Mahón cheese.
✉ **Plaça Nova 4** ☎ **971 48 03
14** 🕒 **Daily 9AM–12PM in summer, weekends only in winter**

Ses Voltes (££)
Charcoal-grilled meats,
wood-fired pizzas and
varieties of *pa amb oli* (toast
with olive oil) are popular at
this busy café-bar in the
pedestrian heart of the city.
✉ **Carrer JM Quadrado 22 (Ses
Voltes)** ☎ **971 38 14 98**
🕒 **Lunch & dinner**

Menú del Día
Most restaurants offer a
menú del día at lunchtime,
and many in the evening
too – a set-price three-
course meal, with water or
wine included. You won't
get much choice (typically
two or three choices for
each course) but what you
do get will be cheap,
freshly cooked and filling.
A full meal, with drinks,
will usually cost about the
same as a main course
from the *à la carte* menu.

Around the Island

Vegetarians

Vegetarians could have a hard time in Menorca – unless they eat fish. *Tapas* bars, however, usually have vegetarian options, including the ever-present *tortilla* (cold potato omelette), and Menorcan pizzas tend to be excellent, cooked the Italian way in a wood-fired oven. Two interesting vegetarian starters are *escalivada*, a mix of grilled vegetables in olive oil, and *tumbet*, a Mallorcan-style ratatouille with potatoes.

Alaior

Es Plans (££)

English-run restaurant just outside Alaior, with fish and chips every night.

✉ **Carretera Maó-Ciutadella** ☎ **971 37 80 78** 🕓 **Dinner daily, Sun lunch**

The Cobblers (££)

Fresh, imaginative Mediterranean cuisine in the garden of a typical Menorcan town house. Booking essential.

✉ **Costa d'en Macari 6** ☎ **971 37 14 00** 🕓 **Apr–Oct: dinner Mon–Sat**

Binibeca Vell

Los Bucaneros (££)

Old-style chiringuito (beach bar) with a bamboo-shaded terrace and a simple menu of salads, sandwiches, burgers and fresh fish.

✉ **Platja de Binibèquer** 🕓 **May–Oct 10–8**

Cala Blanca

Es Caliu (££)

A large and busy restaurant specialising in charcoal-grilled meats.

✉ **Carretera Ciutadella–Cala En Bosc** ☎ **971 38 01 65** 🕓 **Lunch & dinner daily in summer, weekends only in winter**

Il Girasole (££)

Italian restaurant above the beach perfect for families; mini-golf and a waterslide amuse the children while the adults tuck into fresh pasta, pizzas, meat and seafood.

✉ **Cala Blanca** ☎ **971 38 51 68** 🕓 **Lunch & dinner in summer**

Cala En Bosc

Café Balear (££)

This branch of a well-known Ciutadella restaurant specialises in seafood, with dishes ranging from plain grilled lobster to squid in monkfish sauce.

✉ **El Lago** ☎ **608 74 48 16** 🕓 **Lunch & dinner daily in summer**

El Pescador (££)

Fish, seafood, pizzas and a children's menu in a prime position by the marina.

✉ **El Lago** ☎ **971 35 95 39** 🕓 **Lunch & dinner**

Cala Macarella

Susy (££)

This summer restaurant beside the beach serves generous portions of Spanish cuisine such as grilled squid, grilled sole or roast chicken with salad and chips.

✉ **Platja de Macarella** ☎ **971 35 94 67** 🕓 **Daily 10:30–6 in summer**

Cala Mesquida

Es Cap Roig (££)

Fresh fish, simply cooked, in a spectacular setting looking out to sea. This is where the people of Maó come for a treat at weekends.

✉ **Just before the village on the road from Maó** ☎ **971 18 83 83** 🕓 **Lunch & dinner**

Cala Santa Galdana

El Mirador (££)

Perched on a rocky outcrop above one of Menorca's prettiest bays. A wide-ranging menu with the emphasis on seafood.

✉ **Over footbridge from Hotel Audax** ☎ **971 15 45 03** 🕓 **Lunch & dinner**

Es Castell

Aurora (££)

Away from the centre of the resort, this restaurant overlooks the smaller harbour of Cala Corb.

Specialities include beef Wellington, which must be ordered in advance. On warm evenings you can dine outside in a cool courtyard.

✉ **Cala Corb** ☎ 971 36 66 51
🕐 Apr–Oct: Tue–Sun dinner

Bobbie's Bistro Bar (£)

The '3Bs' caters to an expatriate community homesick for hot dogs, beans and chips. Even the fish is imported English cod.

✉ **Cales Fonts 36** ☎ 971 35 13 68 🕐 All day

Bumerang (££)

Long-established restaurant set in an ancient cave. *Paellas*, fish dishes and a good-value set lunch.

✉ **Carrer Sant Josep 9**
☎ 971 35 46 15 🕐 Lunch & dinner

Ca'n Delio (££)

A good place to while away a summer evening eating fresh grilled fish beside the sea.

✉ **Cales Fonts 38** ☎ 971 35 17 11 🕐 Lunch & dinner

El Italiano (££)

Classic Italian cooking in a country house – risottos, pasta with truffles, Spanish and Italian wines. Children can ask for half portions.

✉ **Carretera Sant Felip**
☎ 971 36 53 10 🕐 Dinner only

El Trébol (££)

The best-known fish restaurant in Es Castell, and a night-time haunt of visiting celebrities. Offers a sunny terrace or a shady cave.

✉ **Cales Fonts 43** ☎ 971 36 70 97 🕐 Lunch & dinner

España (£)

The locals come here for solid, unpretentious

Menorcan and Spanish food.

✉ **Carrer Victori 48** ☎ 971 36 32 99 🕐 Lunch & dinner

Irene (££)

This restaurant would be much busier if it were down by the water. Spanish cooking with set menus lunchtime and evening, and a terrace overlooking the harbour at Cales Fonts.

✉ **Carrer Sa Font 1** ☎ 971 35 47 88 🕐 Lunch & dinner

La Caprichosa (££)

Harbourside pizzeria with pasta, meat and fish dishes and a special children's menu. Fish soup a speciality.

✉ **Cales Fonts 44** ☎ 971 36 61 58 🕐 Lunch & dinner

Sa Foganya (££)

Just above the fish restaurants by the harbour, a carnivore's paradise – cured sausages, charcoal-grilled meat and vegetables, steak cooked on a hot slab at your terrace table. The lunchtime menu is good value.

✉ **Carrer Ruiz y Pablo 97**
☎ 971 35 49 50 🕐 Daily 12–12

Siroco (££)

Fresh fish served simply and well in a converted cave beside the harbour. Good-value *menú del día* with a separate children's menu.

✉ **Cales Fonts 39** ☎ 971 36 79 65 🕐 Lunch & dinner

Es Grau
Tarmarindos (££)

Simple fresh fish dishes and *paellas* beside the beach on a wooden terrace built directly over the sea.

✉ **Pas d'es Tamarells 14**
☎ 971 35 94 20 🕐 Lunch & dinner

Wine

Most wines on offer in restaurants are imported from mainland Spain. The best red wines come from Rioja, made from the *tempranillo* grape and aged in oak – those labelled *crianza* are aged for at least a year, *reserva* for two, *gran reserva* for three. Penedés red and white wines from Catalunya are good value, as is *Cava*, Spanish sparkling wine, which comes from the same area.

Caldereta de Langosta

This thick lobster casserole, cooked with onions, tomato, garlic and parsley and served in an earthenware bowl, is the classic seafood dish of Menorca. It comes with thin slices of crispy bread to dip into the soup and a set of tools for tackling the lobster. The best place to eat *caldereta* is at Fornells, where each restaurant has its own recipe. It costs at least 30 euros per person; a cheaper alternative is *caldereta de mariscos* or *caldereta de peix*, with fish or seafood instead of lobster.

Es Mercadal

Ca'n Aguedet (££)

Considered one of the best restaurants on the island for traditional Menorcan cuisine. The owners produce their own wine at a vineyard outside the town.

✉ **Carrer Lepanto 30** ☎ **971 37 53 91** 🕔 **Lunch & dinner**

Ca'n Olga (££)

Authentic Menorcan and Mediterranean cooking in an intimate town house with a pretty summer terrace. Booking essential.

✉ **Pont Na Macarrana** ☎ **971 37 54 59** 🕔 **Dinner daily in summer, weekends only in winter**

Els Arcs (££)

Spanish and Menorcan cuisine on a garden terrace.

✉ **Carretera Maó–Ciutadella** ☎ **971 37 55 38** 🕔 **Lunch & dinner**

Molí des Racó (££)

An old windmill at the top of the main street. In summer meals are served on the delightful terrace.

✉ **Carrer Vicario Fuxà 53** ☎ **971 37 53 92** 🕔 **Lunch & dinner**

Es Migjorn Gran

Ca Na Pilar (££)

Imaginative Mediterranean cooking with a pretty garden terrace.

✉ **Carretera Es Mercadal–Es Migjorn** ☎ **971 37 02 12** 🕔 **Lunch & dinner. Closed Wed**

58 S'Engolidor (££)

Fresh Menorcan cooking in an 18th-century town house with a terrace overlooking a gorge. Booking essential.

✉ **Carrer Major 3** ☎ **971 37 01 93** 🕔 **Dinner only. Closed Mon**

Ferreries

El Gallo (££)

Charcoal grills are a speciality in this 200-year-old farmhouse. The steak with Mahón cheese is known throughout the island.

✉ **Carretera Cala Santa Galdana** ☎ **971 37 30 39** 🕔 **Lunch & dinner. Closed Mon**

Liorna (££)

Arty pizzeria and restaurant; emphasis on modern Catalonian and Italian cuisine.

✉ **Carrer Econom Florit 9** ☎ **971 37 39 12** 🕔 **Dinner only. Closed Tue**

Fornells

Ca'n Miquel (££)

Small restaurant on the waterfront promenade; speciality rice and fish dishes, including the local spiny lobster.

✉ **Passeig Marítim** ☎ **971 37 66 23** 🕔 **Closed all day Mon and Sun dinner**

Cranc Palut (££)

This restaurant at the end of the seafront promenade serves the usual lobster, *paellas* and fish dishes but also has a good selection of meat dishes.

✉ **Passeig Marítim** ☎ **971 37 67 43** 🕔 **Lunch & dinner daily in summer**

El Pescador (££)

Seafood restaurant with wicker chairs on the promenade. Specialities include peppers stuffed with prawns, and lobster from the restaurant's own hatchery.

✉ **Carrer S'Algaret 3** ☎ **971 37 65 38** 🕔 **Lunch & dinner**

Es Cranc (£££)

Local seafood; hidden away in the town so more popular with locals than tourists.

✉ **Carrer Escoles 31** ☎ **971 37 64 42** 🕐 **Lunch & dinner, closed Wed**

Es Pla (£££)

Where King Juan Carlos comes to eat *caldereta de langosta*. Expect to pay at least 50 euros per head.

✉ **Passeig des Pla** ☎ **971 37 66 55** 🕐 **Lunch & dinner**

S'Ancora (££)

One of the best of the fish restaurants directly facing the harbour. Several set menus at different prices, depending whether or not you want to eat lobster.

✉ **Passeig Marítim 8** ☎ **971 37 66 70** 🕐 **Lunch & dinner**

Ses Salines (££)

Fresh fish and seafood, or sandwiches and pizzas, on a terrace overlooking the bay.

✉ **Urbanización Ses Salines** ☎ **971 37 64 91** 🕐 **Lunch & dinner**

Sant Climent

Casino San Clemente (££)

Standard international menu in Menorca's oldest and most popular jazz venue.

✉ **Carrer Sant Jaume 2** ☎ **971 15 34 18** 🕐 **Lunch & dinner. Closed Wed, jazz on Tue**

Es Molí de Foc (£££)

Sophisticated French and Spanish cuisine in a town house with a pretty garden.

✉ **Carrer de Sant Llorens 65** ☎ **971 15 32 22** 🕐 **Lunch Mon–Fri, dinner daily**

Sant Lluís

Biniarroca (£££)

Elegant restaurant in a rural hotel offering fresh Mediterranean cuisine and seasonal produce from their organic gardens. Specialities include ostrich in whisky sauce and duck breast with Grand Marnier. Booking essential.

✉ **Camí Vell de Sant Lluís** ☎ **971 15 00 59** 🕐 **Dinner only. Closed Tue**

El Picadero (££)

British-run carvery and barbecue; very popular with local expats for its Sunday lunch buffet.

✉ **Carretera Maó–Sant Lluís** ☎ **971 36 32 68** 🕐 **Closed Mon lunch**

La Caraba (££)

One of the top restaurants on the island offers modern Mediterranean cuisine in a country house with a summer terrace. Fresh fish and unusual meat dishes like *carpaccio* of ostrich with Mahón cheese.

✉ **S'Uestria 78** ☎ **971 15 06 82** 🕐 **Jun–Sep: Mon–Sat dinner**

La Rueda (££)

Right in the centre of town; a wide selection of *tapas* in the downstairs bar, a restaurant serving Spanish specialities upstairs.

✉ **Carrer Sant Lluís 30** ☎ **971 15 03 49** 🕐 **Lunch & dinner. Closed Tue**

Pan y Vino (£££)

British-run restaurant offering Menorcan specialities such as roast lamb and oven-baked fish in a charming rural house in the village of Torret. Booking essential.

✉ **Torret 52** ☎ **971 15 03 22** 🕐 **Dinner only**

Coffee

Most people drink *café solo* after a meal – short, strong and black, like an espresso. If you want your coffee with milk, ask for *café con leche*; *cortado* is a *café solo* with an extra dash of hot water. The waiter may bring you a glass of brandy or liqueur on the house; ask for a *carajillo* and your coffee will come with brandy already added.

Maó & Ciutadella

Prices

Prices are for a double room, excluding breakfast and VAT:

£ = under 60 euros
££ = 60–120 euros
£££ = over 120 euros

These prices will be much lower if you book as part of a package holiday. Most hotels in the resorts are block-booked by tour operators and it is through them that you will get the cheapest deals.

Maó

Capri (££)
Modern, comfortable, three-star hotel close to Plaça de S'Esplanada.
✉ **Carrer Sant Esteve 8**
☎ **971 36 14 00** 🕐 **All year**

Mirador des Port (££)
Three-star hotel with swimming pool and sea views, 10 minutes' walk from the city centre.
✉ **Carrer Dalt Vilanova 1**
☎ **971 36 00 16** 🕐 **All year**

Orsi (£)
Small, old-fashioned *hostal* in the city centre – the English owner rents out bikes.
✉ **Carrer Infanta 19** ☎ **971 36 47 51** 🕐 **Feb–Nov**

Port Mahón (£££)
The best hotel in the capital, in an imposing colonial-style building overlooking the port. Fabulous gardens and a swimming pool.
✉ **Avinguda Fort de l'Eau 13**
☎ **971 36 26 00** 🕐 **All year**

Ciutadella

Ciutadella (£)
Modest two-star *hostal* in an old terraced house five minutes' walk from the Plaça des Born.
✉ **Carrer Sant Eloy 10** ☎ **971 38 34 62** 🕐 **All year**

Esmeralda (££)
Typical 1960s seaside hotel, beside the Passeig Marítim. Most rooms have sea-facing balconies. Swimming pool, tennis courts and a children's play area.
✉ **Passeig de Sant Nicolau 171**
☎ **971 38 02 50** 🕐 **May–Oct**

Madrid (£)
One-star hotel with a restaurant, swimming pool and garden, convenient for both the city centre and the sea.
✉ **Carrer Madrid 60** ☎ **971 38 03 28** 🕐 **May–Oct**

Oasis (£)
Small, modest *hostal* near the ring road with nine rooms around a central courtyard.
✉ **Carrer Sant Isidre 33**
☎ **971 38 21 97** 🕐 **Apr–Oct**

Paris (£)
Simple rooms in an old-style Menorcan house on the edge of town, close to Cala des Degollador beach.
✉ **Carretera Santandria 4**
☎ **971 38 16 22** 🕐 **Apr–Oct**

Patricia (££)
The best hotel in the city centre, popular with business people. A swimming pool, and mini-bars in every room.
✉ **Passeig de Sant Nicolau 90**
☎ **971 38 55 11** 🕐 **Apr–Oct**

Playa Grande (££)
Small, modern hotel beside the beach at Cala des Degollador, with balconies overlooking the start of the Passeig Marítim.
✉ **Carrer Bisbe Juano 2**
☎ **971 38 24 45** 🕐 **Feb–Dec**

Sant Ignasi (£££)
Former 18th-century summer house turned into a rural hotel with lush gardens, a swimming pool and Anglo–Menorcan furniture.
✉ **Carrer Cala Morell** ☎ **971 38 55 75** 🕐 **Jan–Nov**

Sant Tomàs de Vilanova (£)
A cattle farm outside Ciutadella with three rooms for rent. Horse riding is available.
✉ **Camí Vell, km3** ☎ **971 188 80 51** 🕐 **All year**

Around the Island

Binibeca Vell
Binivell Park (££)
Houses and apartments for rent in this 'Mediterranean fishing village'.
✉ Urbanización Binibeca Vell ☎ 971 15 06 12 ⏰ Apr–Oct

Cala Blanca
Cala Blanca (££)
Large three-star hotel set in pine woods above the beach, with wheelchair access.
✉ Urbanización Cala Blanca ☎ 971 38 04 50 ⏰ May–Oct

Sagítario Playa (££)
One of the few beach hotels to stay open in winter. Tennis courts and disabled access.
✉ Avinguda de la Platja 4 ☎ 971 38 28 77 ⏰ All year

Cala d'Alcaufar
Alcaufar Vell (££)
Rural estate with four large rooms in an old farmhouse, and other rooms in various outbuildings. Small pool. Dinner is served in converted stables on three evenings each week.
✉ Carretera de Cala Alcaufar (7km) ☎ 971 15 18 74 ⏰ Apr–Nov

S'Algar (££)
Modern four-star hotel with impressive facilities; most of the rooms have sea views.
✉ Urbanización S'Algar ☎ 971 15 17 00 ⏰ Apr–Oct

San Luis (££)
Large three-star hotel overlooking the sea, with tennis and mini-golf.
✉ Urbanización S'Algar ☎ 971 15 07 50 ⏰ May–Oct

Xuroy (££)
Charmingly old-fashioned two-star *hostal* with its own landing stage right beside the beach at Cala d'Alcaufar.
✉ Cala d'Alcaufar ☎ 971 15 18 20 ⏰ May–Oct

Cala En Blanes
Almirante Farragut (££)
This massive hotel (880 beds) dominates the small cove of Cala En Forcat. Facilities include swimming pool, tennis courts, mini-golf and bike hire.
✉ Cala En Forcat ☎ 971 38 80 00 ⏰ May–Oct

Cala En Bosc
Cala'n Bosch (££)
Large hotel with rooms overlooking the sea and all the usual facilities.
✉ Urbanización Cala En Bosc ☎ 971 38 70 00 ⏰ May–Oct

La Quinta (£££)
Five-star spa hotel in low-rise colonial-style buildings around a pool. Facilities include bike hire, golf practice area and health centre. A short walk from Son Xoriguer beach, and there are shuttle buses to Ciutadella.
✉ Carrer des Port ☎ 971 38 70 14 ⏰ May–Oct

Cala En Porter
Aquarium (££)
Modern three-star hotel with swimming pool and garden, right beside the beach.
✉ Urbanización Cala En Porter ☎ 971 37 70 77 ⏰ May–Oct

Cala Macarella
Morvedra Nou (£££)
Smart rural hotel close to the south coast beaches with 18 rooms; some in garden villas and others in the 17th-century house. Views stretch to Mallorca on a clear day.
✉ Camí de Macarella (7km) ☎ 971 35 95 21 ⏰ May–Oct

Hotels and *Hostals*
All tourist accommodation in Spain is strictly classified and graded by the government. Hotels are graded from one to five stars according to facilities; *hostals*, with fewer facilities but often just as comfortable, are graded from one to three. At levels below three stars you may have to share a bathroom. Most hotels around the coast are closed throughout the winter; *hostals*, and hotels in the main towns, tend to stay open all year.

Package Holidays
The cheapest accommodation in Menorca is available through tour operators and high-street travel agents, booked as part of a package deal with flights and perhaps car hire. As well as having access to cheaper rates at most hotels, many travel agents offer self-catering accommodation and 'agrotourism' holidays, staying in restored farmhouses and on country estates.

Playa Azul (££)
One-star hotel with its own swimming pool and play area, facing directly on to the beach.
✉ **Passeig Marítim** ☎ **971 37 74 21** 🕔 **May–Oct**

Cala Morell
Biniatram (££)
A 500 year-old farmhouse, with its own private chapel, on a working dairy. Tennis court and swimming pool.
✉ **Carretera de Cala Morell** ☎ **971 38 31 13** 🕔 **All year**

Cala Santa Galdana
Audax (£££)
Luxury four-star beach hotel with a rooftop pool and sea-facing balconies. The hotel's sports centre can arrange everything from bike hire to suba-diving trips.
✉ **Cala Santa Galdana** ☎ **971 15 46 46** 🕔 **Feb–Oct**

Cala Galdana (££)
Comfortable four-star hotel, behind the beach near Algendar gorge; pool, sauna and children's playground.
✉ **Cala Santa Galdana** ☎ **971 15 45 00** 🕔 **Apr–Oct**

Es Castell
Almirante (££)
The former home of the British Admiral Collingwood has become a shrine to 18th-century Menorca, filled with paintings, maps and memorabilia of British rule. Good harbour views.
✉ **Carretera Maó–Es Castell** ☎ **971 35 27 00** 🕔 **May–Oct**

Hamilton (££)
Large, old-fashioned hotel in a quiet, central location, with swimming pool, gym and harbour views.
✉ **Passeig Santa Agueda 6** ☎ **971 36 20 50** 🕔 **All year**

Miramar (££)
This small two-star *hostal* beside the harbour, is well situated for walks along the waterfront at Cala Figuera. Bike hire and a pool.
✉ **Cala Fonduco** ☎ **971 36 29 00** 🕔 **Apr–Oct**

Rey Carlos III (££)
Large three-star hotel with swimming pool and garden overlooking the small harbour at Cala Corb.
✉ **Miranda de Cala Corb** ☎ **971 36 31 00** 🕔 **May–Oct**

Es Mercadal
Jeni (£)
Simple but pleasant one-star *hostal* with a good Menorcan restaurant and a rooftop pool.
✉ **Carrer Miranda del Toro 81** ☎ **971 37 50 59** 🕔 **All year**

Es Migjorn Gran
58 S'Engolidor (££)
Four rooms in a family-run inn overlooking a gorge. The restaurant is one of the most celebrated in Menorca.
✉ **Carrer Major 3** ☎ **971 37 01 93** 🕔 **May–Oct**

Ferreries
Loar (£)
One-star apartment-hotel with its own pool in the centre of town.
✉ **Carrer Reverendo Huguet 2** ☎ **971 37 41 81** 🕔 **All year**

Son Triay Nou (££)
This pink colonial-style farmhouse is now a rural hotel with just four suites, plus a tennis court and swimming pool. The breakfast buffet features typical Menorcan specialities such as local sausages and cheese.
✉ **Carretera Cala Galdana** ☎ **971 15 50 78** 🕔 **All year**

Fornells
Fornells (£££)
Central three-star *hostal* with 17 rooms and a swimming pool. Most rooms have balconies with sea views, and the restaurant serves fresh fish and lobster.

✉ **Carrer Major 17** ☎ **971 37 66 76** 🕐 **All year**

Punta Prima
Insotel Club Punta Prima (£££)
A 5-star holiday village, with low-rise villas and gardens, tennis and squash courts, swimming pools, shops, restaurants, a health centre and children's clubs. The beach is about 300m away.

✉ **Carrer Migjera** ☎ **971 15 92 00** 🕐 **Apr–Oct**

Sant Climent
Matchani Gran (££)
A large farmhouse restored by its British owners to offer luxury accommodation on a working sheep farm. Meals are served in a converted barn, and there is a heated outdoor pool. No children.

✉ **Carretera Sant Climent–Binidali** ☎ **971 15 33 00** 🕐 **Apr–Oct**

Sant Lluís
Biniali (££)
Eleven individual rooms in an old farmhouse southwest of town. Swimming pool.

✉ **Carretera S'Uestrà 50** ☎ **971 15 17 24** 🕐 **Apr–Oct**

Biniarroca (£££)
A 16th-century farmhouse lovingly restored and filled with art and antiques. Some of the 12 rooms have their own private garden and pool. A peaceful, child-free retreat.

✉ **Camí Vell de Sant Lluís** ☎ **971 15 00 59** 🕐 **Mar–Oct**

Son Tretze (££)
This 18th-century farmhouse at the entrance to Sant Lluís opened in 2000. There are eight rooms and a garden with gazebo and swimming pool. No children.

✉ **Carrer Binifadet 20** ☎ **971 15 09 43** 🕐 **All year**

Sant Tomàs
Santo Tomàs (£££)
Four-star hotel close to the beach, with 85 rooms and a large swimming pool.

✉ **Urbanización Santo Tomàs** ☎ **971 37 00 25** 🕐 **May–Oct**

Son Bou
Jardín de Menorca (£££)
Luxury four-star apartment-hotel in the resort of Sant Jaume Mediterrani.

✉ **Urbanización Torre Solí Nou** ☎ **971 37 80 40** 🕐 **May–Oct**

Sol Milanos (££)
One of the pair of concrete monstrosities that dominate the east end of the beach (the other is Sol Pinguinos). The rooms have sea-facing balconies and the hotels share facilities.

✉ **Platja Son Bou** ☎ **971 37 11 00** 🕐 **May–Oct**

Son Valentín Menorca (££)
Four-star 'aparthotel' in pine woods above the sea with rooms specially adapted for visitors with disabilities.

✉ **Urbanización Torre Solí Nou** ☎ **971 37 27 48** 🕐 **May–Oct**

Son Parc
Sol Parc (££)
Two-star apartment hotel in a village built around Menorca's only golf course.

✉ **Urbanización Son Parc** ☎ **971 18 81 51** 🕐 **May–Oct**

Camping
Menorca has two official campsites, at Son Bou (☎ 971 37 26 05) and S'Atalaia (☎ 971 37 30 95), 4km from Ferreries on the road to Cala Santa Galdana. Son Bou (🕐 Apr–Sep), S'Atalaia (🕐 Jun–Sep). Unofficial camping is forbidden on beaches, within 1km of a town or 50m of a road. You may camp on farmland with the owner's consent, but never light fires.

Food & Drink

Markets

The two main food markets, in the Carmelite cloisters in Maó and Plaça Libertat in Ciutadella, are open every morning from Monday to Saturday. Most towns in Menorca also have a weekly market, with clothes and craft stalls set up around the main square. Market days are:

Maó – Tue, Sat
Ciutadella – Fri, Sat
Alaior – Mon, Thu
Es Castell – Mon, Wed
Es Migjorn Gran – Wed
Ferreries – Tue
Es Mercadal – Sun
Fornells – Thu

There is also a weekly farmers' market, held in the main square of Ferreries on Saturday mornings. Local farmers sell bread, cheese, honey and fresh produce and there are also pottery and craft stalls and folk-dancing displays.

Good buys include Mahón cheese, Xoriguer gin, Spanish wines and brandy, herbal liqueurs, almond biscuits and olive oil.

Maó

Colmado La Palma
Delicatessen with a good selection of Mahón farmhouse cheeses as well as Menorcan sausages, biscuits, gin and Spanish wines.
✉ **Costa de Sa Plaça 15**
☎ **971 36 34 63**

Vallès
Arty pastries and chocolate on Maó's upmarket shopping street.
✉ **Costa de Sa Plaça 19**
☎ **971 36 34 88**

Xoriguer
Waterfront distillery producing gin and gin-based liqueurs (➤ 37).
✉ **Moll de Ponent 93**
☎ **971 36 21 97**

Xoriguer
The distillery also has a shop in the centre of town, with a good variety of Spanish wines as well as local gin.
✉ **Plaça del Carme 16**
☎ **971 36 26 11**

Ciutadella

El Diamante
Chocolate creations in remarkable designs.
✉ **Carrer Es Quadrado 41 (Ses Voltes)** ☎ **971 38 09 40**

Miguel Bagur
Pastry shop specialising in boxed *ensaimadas* and a range of home-made biscuits.
✉ **Carrer JM Quadrado 8 (Ses Voltes)** ☎ **971 38 06 40**

Ses Industries
Wines, liqueurs, cheese in olive oil plus shelves full of kitsch souvenirs in this Aladdin's cave near the cathedral.
✉ **Carrer Santa Clara 4**
☎ **971 38 28 82**

Alaior

Coinga
The leading producer of Mahón cheese; the factory shop sells several varieties, ranging from young to very mature.
✉ **Carrer Es Mercadal 8**
☎ **971 37 12 27**

La Payesa
Another factory outlet selling Mahón cheese.
✉ **Carrer des Banyer 64**
☎ **971 37 10 72**

Es Mercadal

Ca'n Pons
Es Mercadal is known for its tasty almond macaroons, and this is one of the best establishments to purchase them.
✉ **Carrer Nou 13** ☎ **971 37 52 58**

Los Claveles
Pastry-shop specialising in interesting Menorcan and Arabic-style biscuits and sweets.
✉ **Carrer Nou 9** ☎ **971 15 40 64**

Ferreries

Hort de Sant Patrici
This dairy farm just outside Ferreries offers tastings of unpasteurised farmhouse cheese as well as a cheese museum and the chance to see Mahón cheese being made.
✉ **Camino Ruma, 1km north of Ferreries** ☎ **971 37 37 02**

Arts, Books & Gifts

The best hunting-grounds for unusual gifts are the boutiques along the waterfront in Maó and in the back streets of Maó and Ciutadella. Carrer Seminari in Ciutadella has some small shops specialising in modern art, jewellery and antiques. A craft market is held here and in the surrounding streets on Thursday evenings in summer. There are more craft shops in the Centre d'Artesania beneath the Molí des Comte (► 40).

Art and Crafts

Maó
Lora Buzón
This pottery workshop will make items to order and ship them anywhere in the world. It also has a good selection of 'ecological' T-shirts and cotton clothing manufactured in Menorca.
✉ **Moll de Ponent 10**
☎ **971 36 36 85**

S'Alambic
Francesc Lora's pottery and a wide range of crafts and souvenirs are on sale at this waterfront shop.
✉ **Moll de Ponent 36**
☎ **971 35 03 03**

Ciutadella
Huit
Antiques, jewellery and regional Spanish pottery beside the harbour.
✉ **Carrer Marina 73**
☎ **971 48 27 47**

Es Castell
S'Escopinya
Harbourside boutique specialising in Lladró porcelain.
✉ **Cales Fonts 1**
☎ **971 36 76 92**

Es Mercadal
Galeria del Sol
Art gallery featuring work by foreign artists in Menorca.
✉ **Via Ronda 28**
☎ **971 15 40 07**

Es Migjorn Gran
Galeria Migjorn Gran
Watercolours by British artist Graham Byfield, who lives in the village, and by other local artists.
✉ **Carrer Sant Llorenc 12**
☎ **971 37 03 64**

Books

Maó
Fundació
The best selection of books in Maó, including books on Menorca in English and German.
✉ **Costa de Sa Plaça 14**
☎ **971 36 35 43**

Ciutadella
Samatha
A New Age bookshop selling candles and incense, hidden among the many boutiques on an elegant shopping street.
✉ **Carrer Seminari 22**
☎ **971 38 41 91**

Gifts

Es Mercadal
Sa Farinera
The best of the large shopping emporiums that are strung out along the Maó to Ciutadella road. Set in an old flour mill, the complex includes an industrial museum as well as shops selling pottery, clothing and toys.
✉ **Carretera Maó–Ciutadella, km20** ☎ **971 15 43 08**
🕐 **May–Oct: daily 10–8**

Opening Hours

Most shops are open from around 10–1:30 and 5–8 Monday to Friday, and on Saturday mornings. Supermarkets and souvenir shops in the resorts will often stay open for longer hours, and the SYP supermarkets in Maó, Ciutadella and Sant Lluis are open from 9–9 Monday to Saturday and on Sunday mornings. Many smaller shops, especially in tourist areas, close throughout the winter.

Leather, Jewellery & Fashions

Shoes
Menorca's shoe industry was founded in the 19th century by Jerónimo Cabrisas, a businessman who emigrated to Cuba and returned to set up an export trade in shoes. At one stage, almost 40 per cent of the population was employed in shoemaking and the industry is still one of the most important on the island. Prices are good if you shop around, and the leather used in the best shoes is wonderfully soft and supple.

Leather and Fashions

Maó

Complements
As well as leather bags and shoes, this shop has a good range of children's clothes.
✉ Carrer del Rosari 3 ☎ 971 36 59 81

Jaime Mascaro
Maó branch of Menorca's best-known shoe manufacturer; the shop also sells leather jackets and bags.
✉ Carrer Ses Moreres 29
☎ 971 36 05 68

Looky
Leather and suede waistcoats, handbags and belts, designer T-shirts and locally made shoes.
✉ Carrer Ses Moreres 43
☎ 971 36 06 48

Marisa
Elegant boutique on Maó's smartest shopping street, with a fine selection of leather bags.
✉ Costa de Sa Plaça
☎ 971 36 27 63

Mark's
Handbags, belts, suitcases and jackets, sold at two shops in the city centre.
✉ S'Arravaleta 18 and Costa de Sa Plaça 38 ☎ 971 36 26 60 and 971 36 56 25

Patricia
Quality shoes and other fashion accessories by a well-known designer.
✉ Carrer Ses Moreres 31
☎ 971 36 91 78

Pou Nou
These Menorcan designer T-shirts are sold all over the island, but the factory shop on Maó's industrial estate has the best prices.
✉ S'Olivar 19, Poligon Industrial ☎ 971 36 91 59
🕓 Tue and Thu 9:30–2

Riccy
Up-market boutique featuring high-class leather and jewellery.
✉ Carrer Nou 17 ☎ 971 36 57 84

Vives
Leather shoes and accessories.
✉ S'Arravaleta 16
☎ 971 36 28 46

Ciutadella

Blau Mari
This fashionable shop in the vaults of the Palau Salord has a wide range of shoes, espadrilles, leather articles and colourful T-shirts.
✉ Carrer Major del Born 11
☎ 971 48 10 95

Ca Sa Pollaca
This shop has been selling hand-made leather shoes and sandals since 1899; they have a lovely selection of *abarcas* (rubber-soled sandals) for children.
✉ Carrer JM Quadrado 10 (Ses Voltes) ☎ 971 38 22 23

Looky
A wide range of shoes and fashion accessories in leather and suede.
✉ Carrer JM Quadrado 14 (Ses Voltes) ☎ 971 38 19 32

Munper
Huge factory shop on the outskirts of town selling good quality leather goods such as handbags and shoes.
✉ Carretera Maó–Ciutadadella, km42
☎ 971 38 03 50

Patricia
Another branch of Patricia's empire, on the road out of town.

✉ **Carretera Cala Santandria**
☎ **971 38 50 56**

Torres
A large selection of men's and women's shoes, from cheap trainers to high-class leather.

✉ **Camí de Maó 35**
☎ **971 38 05 00**

Es Castell
S'Abarca
This workshop on the harbour steps produces hand-made *abaracas* (Menorcan sandals). There is another branch in Maó.

✉ **Baixada de Cales Fonts; also at Moll de Llevant 21, Maó**
☎ **971 35 34 62**

Es Mercadal
G. Servera
Old-fashioned craftsman producing the local sandals known as *abarcas*, with leather uppers and a sole made out of recycled rubber tyres. Get here early in your holiday and you can have shoes made to measure before you leave.

✉ **Avinguda Metge Camps 3**
☎ **971 37 53 84**

Ferreries
Calzados Ferrerias
Ferreries is the centre of shoe production in Menorca and this shop sells the products of a local factory.

✉ **Avinguda Verge del Monte Toro 36** ☎ **971 15 52 48**

Jaime Mascaro
Large factory shop beside the Maó–Ciutadella highway, representing the best-known name in Menorcan shoes.

✉ **Carretera Maó–Ciutadella**
☎ **971 37 40 27**

Jewellery

Maó
Anna
Gold, silver, natural and atificial pearls are all on sale at this smart jewellery shop.

✉ **Carrer Ses Moreres 46**
☎ **971 36 33 83**

Lopez
A wide selection of silver and jewellery, including Majórica pearls from Mallorca.

✉ **Carrer Ses Moreres 58 & 60**
☎ **971 36 04 78**

Luxor
Costume jewellery and other accessories on the corner of Plaça de S'Esplanada.

✉ **Carrer Ses Moreres 61**
☎ **971 36 72 13**

Ciutadella
Carles
Old-fashioned jewellers' shop in the heart of the old city.

✉ **Carrer Santa Clara 16**
☎ **971 38 07 34**

Joies
Smart jewellery shop in the pedestrian part of town.

✉ **Carrer de Maó 6** ☎ **971 38 33 11**

Joyería Anglada
Jewellery, silver, gold and Majórica pearls under the arches in Ses Voltes.

✉ **Carrer JM Quadrado 23 (Ses Voltes)** ☎ **971 38 15 48**

Joyería Delfin
Costume jewellery plus art and antiques in one of Ciutadella's smartest shopping streets.

✉ **Carrer Seminari 16**
☎ **971 38 08 88**

Costume Jewellery
One of Menorca's leading industries is the manufacture of costume jewellery, using common metals which are coated with silver or gold and finished with imitation stones. The effect is to create something extravagant, yet without the expense of precious metal or gems. Most of the costume jewellery produced in Menorca is exported to South America, but there are still bargains to be had – especially at the two annual fairs of costume jewellery, SEBIME, held in Maó's trade fair centre in April and September (☎ 971 36 03 13).

Children's Attractions

Looking After Children

Small children are particularly vulnerable to the sun and need to be protected; apply a high-factor sun block regularly, especially after swimming. If you need a child seat in your hire car, make sure to book it in advance and check it carefully on arrival. The same goes for cots and high-chairs in hotels and apartments. Finally, don't forget to check that your balcony railings are secure.

Menorca is a very child-friendly society. Like other Mediterranean people, the Spanish are known for their love of children and no-one is going to complain if you take your child out to a good restaurant in the evening.

Menorca is ideal for family holidays. A large number of hotels have children's nurseries and baby-sitting services and package-tour operators will lay on children's activities during the day. Every town and beach resort has at least one children's playground, and very often these are found in hotels too. Some hotels also have mini-golf circuits and children's pools. Make sure you ask your hotel or travel agent about these facilities before you go.

Most children are happy just being on the beach – and fortunately Menorca has a wealth of child-friendly beaches, with safe, shallow water and Red Cross posts in case of emergency. It is easy to buy beach toys; for bigger thrills, take the children for a ride on a pedaloe or an inflatable banana. Do remember, though, that children are especially vulnerable to dangerous conditions, and never let them go into the sea when the red danger flag is flying.

Children will enjoy the 'road trains' that travel around the major resorts such as Son Bou, Cala Santa Galdana, Cala En Blanes, Cala En Bosc and Punta Prima in summer. The following is a list of other activities which will particularly appeal to children. All of them only operate during the summer season, usually from May to October.

Beaches

The following beaches are particularly suitable for children. All have shallow water, plenty of sand, and are easily reached by car. You can rent pedaloes at all of these beaches in summer; some of the larger ones (such as Cala Santa Galdana and Son Parc) also have canoes and motor boats for hire.

Arenal d'en Castell
Binibeca
Cala Blanca
Cala d'Alcaufar
Cala En Porter
Cala Santa Galdana
Cala Santandría
Es Grau
Son Bou
Son Parc

Boat Trips

Children always enjoy the thrill of the open water and there are numerous boat excursions around the Menorcan coast in summer. Services vary throughout the season so it is best to ask at your hotel or look out for notices on the quayside. A popular option is a full-day trip to a cove that cannot be reached by road; the price often includes lunch, usually a *paella* cooked on the beach. Another option is to charter your own yacht or motor boat and simply set off to explore.

Popular boat trips include:
Cala En Bosc to Arenal de Son Saura and Cala En Turqueta.
Cala Santa Galdana to Cala Trebalúger.
Ciutadella to Arenal de Son Saura and Cala En Turqueta.
Es Grau to Illa d'en Colom.
Port d'Addaia to Fornells.

Animals

Alaior

Ostriches de Menorca
Menorca's only ostrich ranch is open to the public for visits during the breeding season (by appointment only).
✉ **Carretera Alaior–Es Migjorn Gran** ☎ **971 18 83 46**

Picadero Menorca
This ranch on the outskirts of Alaior offers pony rides and rides in a horse and cart.
✉ **Carretera Son Bou** ☎ **608 32 35 66** 🚌 **Buses from Maó and Alaior in summer**

Ferreries

Club Escola Menorquina
The equestrian show here features carriage rides, dressage displays and performances of prancing and rearing horses. Children can go for a ride in a donkey-cart during the interval.
✉ **Carretera Cala Galdana, km0.5** ☎ **971 37 34 97**
🕐 **May–Oct: Wed & Sun 8:30PM**

Son Martorellet
Another show featuring elegant displays of horse-riding and equestrian ballet, with a miniature train ride for kids.
✉ **Carretera Cala Galdana, km1.5** ☎ **609 04 94 93**
🕐 **May–Oct: Tue & Thu 8:30PM**

Restaurants

Cala Blanca

Il Girasole
The attractions here are the giant waterslide and the crazy golf course, ideal for keeping children entertained while you enjoy Italian food overlooking the beach.
✉ **Cala Blanca**
☎ **971 38 51 68**

Cala Santa Galdana

Tobogán
Pizzeria featuring mini-golf, a playground, a waterslide and a small pool.
✉ **Passeig del Riu** ☎ **971 15 46 16**

Adventure Parks

Cala En Blanes

Aquapark
This waterpark near Ciutadella will keep children entertained for hours, with waterslides, trampolines, bouncy castles, mini-golf, video games, go-karts and a pizzeria.
✉ **Avinguda de los Delfines** ☎ **971 38 82 51** 🕐 **May–Oct: daily 10:30–6**

Son Bou

Club San Jaime
This is the top children's attraction on the island – a wealth of activities to keep little ones amused, including a swimming pool, a water-chute and a remarkable interlocking wooden maze that can be rearranged to get harder as you go along. The whole complex is arranged around a series of attractively landscaped gardens with views over the marshes and out to sea.
✉ **Sant Jaume Mediterrani** ☎ **971 37 27 87** 🕐 **May–Oct: daily 10–7**

Son Parc

Hort de Llucaitx Park
Countryside recreation centre with a wide range of activities for kids of all ages – pony-trekking, bike hire, mini-golf, cart rides, playgrounds and a pool.
✉ **Carretera Maó–Fornells, km17** ☎ **629 39 28 94**
🕐 **May–Oct: daily 10–8**

Family Outings
As well as the attractions listed here, children will enjoy the trotting races at Maó and Ciutadella (➤ 113), the Molí de Dalt windmill at Sant Lluís (➤ 83) and the boat tours of Maó harbour (➤ 23).

Art Galleries, Cinemas & Theatres

What's On?
To find out what's on while you're staying, ask at your hotel or the tourist offices in Maó and Ciutadella, or check the listings in the daily paper *Menorca* and the English-language monthly *Roqueta*. In Ciutadella you can also look at the billboards which are displayed in Ses Voltes. Everything starts late – plays at around 9PM, films at 10, and music at any time up to midnight.

Art Galleries

Maó
Sala de Cultura La Caixa
A gallery in the heart of the pedestrian shopping quarter hosting temporary exhibitions of modern art.
✉ Carrer Nou 25

Sala de Cultura Sa Nostra
Art exhibitions in the former convent of Sant Antoni.
✉ S'Arraval 32 ☎ 971 36 68 54

Ciutadella
Sala de Cultura Sa Nostra
Exhibition rooms and educational activities.
✉ Carrer Santa Clara 9 ☎ 971 48 06 86

Església del Roser
Occasional art exhibitions are held inside this restored 17th-century baroque church.
✉ Carrer del Roser ☎ 971 38 10 50

Museu del Pintor Torrent
Collection of works by José Torrent (➤ 41).
✉ Carrer Rafel 11 ☎ 971 34 04 82 🕐 Mon–Sat 11–1, 7:30–9:30 in summer

Es Migjorn Gran
Galeria Migjorn Gran
Exhibitions of work by the British watercolour artist Graham Byfield and other local artists.
✉ Carrer Sant Llorenc 12 ☎ 971 37 03 64 🕐 Apr–Oct: Mon–Sat 10–1, 7–9

Cinemas

Maó
Cine Alcazar
✉ Carrer Santa Ana 27 ☎ 971 36 34 06

Cine Salón Victoria
✉ Carrer Sant Roc 24 ☎ 971 36 90 93

Sala Augusta
Occasional open-air films in summer.
✉ Carrer Santiago Ramón i Cajal 11 ☎ 971 36 46 07

Ciutadella
Casino 17 de Gener
✉ Avinguda de la Constitució 18 ☎ 971 48 26 57

Cinema des Born
Films are frequently shown in the city's theatre.
✉ Plaça des Born ☎ 971 38 49 13

Alaior
Centro Cultural Alaior
The Cine Club in Alaior's cultural centre shows occasional films on Tuesdays and at weekends in winter.
✉ Plaça Constitució 1 ☎ 971 37 10 24

Theatres

Maó
Teatre Principal
An elegant newly restored opera house with films, plays and a spring opera season. For the best views book a seat in one of the 80 boxes.
✉ Costa d'en Deià 46 ☎ 971 35 57 76

Ciutadella
Teatre Municipal des Born
The city's theatre in a 19th-century neo-classical building in a corner of the Born.
✉ Plaça des Born ☎ 971 38 49 13

Music & Nightlife

Most of the late-night action in summer takes place in and around the big tourist resorts, where foreign-owned bars and pubs offer familiar accents and familiar beer. To meet locals head for some of these more established bars in the main towns.

Bars and Clubs

Maó

Akelarre
This waterfront bar attracts a sophisticated yachting crowd with its laid-back music and 'maritime cocktails'.
✉ Moll de Ponent 42 ☎ 971 36 85 20 🕐 Daily 8AM–5AM

Café Baixamar
Late-night meeting place of the young and trendy, on the waterfront.
✉ Moll de Ponent 17 ☎ 971 36 58 96 🕐 Daily 8AM–2AM

Icaro
Loud music and latenight *copas* (drinks) at one of the longest established harbour bars.
✉ Moll de Llevant 46 ☎ 971 36 97 35 🕐 Daily 8PM–4AM

Nashville
'Beer and soundhouse' on the seafront with loud music and German and American food.
✉ Moll de Llevant 147 ☎ 971 36 79 56 🕐 Daily 9AM–3AM

Pierro
Large terrace bar with harbour views, open day and night.
✉ Moll de Llevant 218 ☎ 971 35 43 60 🕐 Daily 10AM–late

Salsa
Trendy nightspot with cool Latin sounds, close to the ferry port.
✉ Moll de Ponent 29

Ciutadella

Asere
Salsa club with Cuban music and cocktails – go late.
✉ Port de Ciutadella
☎ 609 67 26 10 🕐 Daily 11AM–4AM in summer, weekends only in winter

Es Castell

Es Cau
Bring your own instruments to this music bar, situated inside a cave. The emphasis is on folk music, including traditional fishermen's songs.
✉ Cala Corb 🕐 Daily from 10PM

Piano Bar
Cool, late-night cocktail bar.
✉ Carrer Sant Ignasi II
☎ 971 36 40 22 🕐 Daily from 10:30PM in summer, weekends only in winter

Sant Climent

Casino San Clemente
Menorca's oldest jazz venue, with a large expat following. Sessions are held throughout the summer and visitors are encouraged to join in.
✉ Carrer Sant Jaume 2
☎ 971 15 34 18 🕐 Jazz nights Apr–Oct: Tue 9:30PM–1AM

Casino

Maó

Casino Marítim
Menorca's only casino situated close to the Port Mahón hotel, with a terrace overlooking the habour. Blackjack, poker and American roulette can be played. Passports are required to enter the casino; smart dress is expected.
✉ Moll de Llevant 287
☎ 971 36 49 62 🕐 Casino: daily 7PM–5AM; slot machines: 11AM–5AM

Classical Music Festivals
As well as Maó's spring opera season, there are international festivals of young musicians each summer in Maó and Ciutadella. Organ recitals are held daily from June to October in Maó's Santa Maria church, and a series of Easter concerts takes place in the main churches in Maó, Ciutadella, Alaior, Es Mercadal and Ferreries. Concerts are also held in summer in the cloisters and chapel of the Museu Diocesà in Ciutadella.

Discos

Cova d'en Xoroi
This bar and disco is set inside a natural cave, high in the cliff-face above the sea. There are numerous stairways and rock platforms, and a dance floor precariously overlooking the sea. Open during the day for drinks, it turns into a disco at night and gets busy after midnight. There is an interesting Arabic legend attached to the cave (➤ 58).

By their very nature, discos come and go – what's in this year will already be *passé* by next, and changes of name and image are essential to keep the punters rolling in. Most of the larger resorts will have a disco of one kind or another, sometimes based in a hotel nightclub, and the only thing to do is to ask around or listen out for the disco beat. These are a few of the island's more established discos, or *salas de fiestas* ('party halls'). Most are open nightly throughout the peak tourist season, but only at weekends – if at all – in winter. They mostly get busy around midnight.

Maó
Karai
Young, late-night disco in a cliff face on the outskirts of Maó.
✉ **Sa Sinia d'es Muret**
☎ **971 36 36 45**

Si
Cool late-night spot with a name which means 'yes'. Or should that be yes, yes, yes…
✉ **Carrer Verge de Gràcia 16**
☎ **971 36 00 04**

Ciutadella
Lateral
The old warehouses around the Pla de Sant Joan (the open space behind the marina) are home to numerous clubs and discos, which get busy around midnight and continue into the small hours. This is probaby the best-known. Just choose the music and the décor that suits your style – they change from year to year.

✉ **Pla de Sant Joan 9**
☎ **971 38 53 28**

Cala En Blanes
Danzas
Popular and lively disco at the heart of the extensive Los Delfines tourist complex around the bay of Cala En Forcat.
✉ **Urbanización Los Delfines**
☎ **971 38 30 45**

Cala En Porter
Cova d'en Xoroi
Menorca's most unusual disco (see panel).
✉ **Urbanización Cala En Porter**
☎ **971 37 73 36**

Son Bou
San Jaime
Part of the Club San Jaime complex in the neighbouring resort of Sant Jaume Mediterrani.
✉ **Urbanización Sant Jaume**
☎ **971 37 27 87**

Street Parties
Large, outdoor street parties featuring discos and live music are a feature of all Menorca's main festivals (➤ 116). During the festival of La Verge del Gràcia, in Maó in September, outdoor concerts are held each evening in various venues including Plaça de S'Esplanada, Plaça Miranda and the harbourside. These are a great way of meeting local people and soaking up the atmosphere of a Menorcan party. For details, check in the local paper or simply ask around at festival time in the local bars.
There are also occasional rock concerts at Maó's sports stadium, Polideportivo Municipal (☎ 971 36 76 61). You will find details in the local newspaper.

Spectator &
Participatory Sport

Cricket

Sant Lluís
Menorca Cricket Club
The British expatriate community in Menorca keep their national game going, with games against visiting sides from Britain and the Mallorca at weekends in summer. Tourists are welcome to watch, or to join in with the open games that take place on Wednesdays in July and August from 10AM.
✉ **Urbanización Biniparell, Sant Lluís (signposted from the Sant Lluís–Binidali road)**

Football

Maó
Estadio Mahonés
Sporting Mahón are hardly one of Spain's big-name teams but if you want to see them in action, they are at home on alternate Sunday afternoons throughout the season, which runs from September to June.
✉ **Carrer Virgen de Gràcia 21**
☎ **971 36 31 70**

Golf

Son Parc
Club Son Parc
Menorca's only golf course, a short 9-hole course, opened in 1977 and is being extended to 18 holes. Tuition is available and you can hire clubs and equipment.
✉ **Urbanización Son Parc**
☎ **971 18 88 75**

Horse-racing

Maó/Sant Lluís
Hipódromo de Maó
Trotting races (see panel) are held here throughout the year, on Saturday evenings in summer and Sunday mornings in winter.
✉ **Carretera Maó–Sant Lluís**
☎ **971 36 57 30**

Ciutadella/Cala En Blanes
Hipódromo de Ciutadella
Trotting races held on Sunday, April to December, at 6PM.
✉ **Torre del Ram, Cala En Blanes** ☎ **971 38 80 38**

Horse Riding

Horse and pony hire and excursions are available from the following centres.

Ciutadella
Picadero Sant Tomás
✉ **Camí Vell, km3**
☎ **971 18 80 51**

Alaior
Picadero Menorca
✉ **Carretera Son Bou**
☎ **608 32 35 66**

Cala d'Alcaufar
Picadero Es Boeret
✉ **Urbanización S'Algar**
☎ **971 15 10 49**

Sant Climent
Picadero Binixica
✉ **Carretera Cala En Porter**
☎ **971 15 30 71**

Multi-activity

Cala Santa Galdana
Audax Sports & Nature
The beach hut beneath the Hotel Audax offers a wide variety of sporting activities from canoeing and fishing to tennis, golf, scuba-diving and beach volleyball. In addition, there is a regular programme of boat trips, cycle rides and guided walks.
✉ **Passeig del Riu** ☎ **971 15 45 48** 🕐 **Apr–Oct**

Trotting

Trotting has been popular in the Balearic Islands for at least 200 years; at one time neighbouring villages used to hold trotting races against each other. The jockey sits in a small cart behind the horse and has to prevent his horse from breaking into a gallop. A handicap system ensures that weaker horses get a head start on the others. The trotting races in Maó and Ciutadella at weekends make a great excuse for a family day out with a picnic – and a few bets on the side.

Watersports

Sailing in Menorca
The calm waters around Menorca are perfect for sailing – there are no tides, few currents and the only real hazard is the *tramuntana* wind. There are long, sheltered bays at Maó, Fornells and Port d'Addaia and smaller inlets at Es Grau and Ciutadella; all of these are suitable for novice sailors but only experienced hands should tackle the open sea. You can charter yachts at any of the nautical clubs.

Sailing

Nautical clubs

Maó
Club Marítimo
✉ Moll de Llevant 287
☎ 971 36 50 22

Ciutadella
Club Náutico
✉ Camí de Baix ☎ 971 38 39 19

Es Castell
Club Náutico
✉ Cales Fonts ☎ 971 36 58 84

Fornells
Club Náutico
✉ Passatge des Pla
☎ 971 37 66 03

Cala En Bosc
Club Deportivo
✉ Marina ☎ 971 38 71 71

Repair Facilities

Maó
Pedro's Boat Centre
✉ Moll de Ponent 75
☎ 971 36 69 68

Sailing Schools

The following offer tuition in sailing and windsurfing.

Cala en Bosc
Surf 'n' Sail Menorca
✉ Platja de Son Xoriguer
☎ 971 38 70 90

Fornells
Servinàutic Menorca
✉ Carrer Major 27
☎ 971 37 66 36

Windsurf Fornells
✉ Platja de Fornells
☎ 971 18 81 50

Scuba Diving

Diving Schools

Ciutadella
Sports Massanet
✉ Moll Commercial 66
☎ 971 48 21 86

Arenal d'en Castell
La Sirena
✉ Plaça del Mar 2 ☎ 971 35 85 22

Binibeca Vell
Cala Torret
✉ Urbanización Cala Torret
☎ 971 18 85 28

Cala d'Alcaufar
Club S'Algar
✉ Urbanización S'Algar
☎ 971 15 06 01

Cala En Bosc
Crystal Seas Scuba
✉ Centro Comercial 11 & 12
☎ 971 38 70 38

Hotel Club Falcó
✉ Urbanización Cala En Bosc
☎ 971 38 70 70

Sub Menorca
✉ Son Xoriguer ☎ 971 38 70 69

Cala Santa Galdana
Diving Center
✉ Hotel Gavilanes ☎ 971 15 45 45

Cala Santandría
Hotel Poseidón
✉ Platja Santandría ☎ 971 38 26 44

Es Castell
Florit Sub
Carrer Gran 83 ☎ 971 36 52 59

Fornells
Menorca Diving Club

✉ **Passeig Marítim 98**
☎ 971 37 64 12

Servinàutic Menorca
✉ **Carrer Major 27** ☎ 971 37 66 36

Port d'Addaia
Ulmo Diving Addaia
✉ **Zona Comercial** ☎ 971 35 90 05

Punta Prima
Hotel Pueblo Menorca
✉ **Punta Prima** ☎ 971 15 90 70

Swimming
Most resort hotels have outdoor swimming pools and a few have heated indoor pools. Swimming in the sea is generally safe but beware of currents in the remoter coves and look for the safety flag system at those beaches manned by the Red Cross. It is generally warm enough to swim in the sea from June to October. A few Menorcan beaches have been awarded the European Union Blue Flag, which means it is safe, clean and well-kept. Blue Flag beaches include Arenal d'en Castell, Binibeca, Cala Santa Galdana, Cala Santandría, Es Grau and Son Xoriguer.

Polideportivo Municipal
Maó's sports stadium includes Menorca's only public indoor swimming pool, open throughout the year.
✉ **Polígon Industrial**
☎ 971 36 76 61

Water-skiing
There is not much water-skiing available round the island, with keen visitors being more or less confined to Cala d'Alcaufar and Fornells. You can also water-ski behind your own motorboat, but it is essential to show respect to other sea-users. Water-skiing is forbidden in Maó and Ciutadella harbours. The following clubs offer tuition for beginners.

Cala d'Alcaufar
Club S'Algar
✉ **Urbanización S'Algar**
☎ 971 15 06 01

Fornells
Servinàutic Menorca
✉ **Carrer Major 27** ☎ 971 37 66 36

Windsurfing
Windsurfing boards and equipment are available for hire at several of the larger resorts; the place to ask is usually at the beach bar. Tuition is sometimes available as well – the sheltered coves and bays around the island create ideal conditions for beginners, particularly in the Bay of Fornells. The sailing schools listed above provide instruction in windsurfing as well.

Beach Activities
At most of the larger beaches it is possible to rent a range of equipment for fun and games out on the water. Most popular are pedaloes, which are ideal for the whole family to enjoy. Canoes and kayaks are also widely available. For a real adrenalin rush, you can go out on a jet-ski, or take a banana ride on a giant inflatable banana as it is towed at speed through the water. Make sure you wear a life-jacket.

Diving in Menorca
The clear waters in many of Menorca's bays make for excellent diving. Besides the wealth of marine life, there are also numerous caves to explore and shipwrecks to discover off Cala Mesquida, Punta Nati and Son Bou. Diving is expensive – a single dive might cost 30 euros – and you are required to take out both insurance and membership of the Spanish diving federation. Remember, it can be dangerous to fly less than 24 hours after diving.

What's On When

Festivals in Menorca

Most of Menorca's festivals are Christian in origin, with touches of pagan ritual and a passion for horses introduced by the Arabs. Each town has its own *festa*, in honour of its patron saint – a week of parties, concerts and sporting events culminates in a final weekend of festivities, with horseback processions, music and dancing and a midnight firework display in the main square.

January

Los Reyes Magos (5 Jan): The Three Kings arrive by boat in Maó to deliver Christmas presents to the city's children the next day. Similar events take place across the island.

Sant Antoni Abad (16–17 Jan): Bonfires, dancing and fancy dress parties in Maó, Es Castell and elsewhere on 16 January; on 17 January, following a Mass in Ciutadella cathedral, there is a horseback procession to Plaça Alfons III.

March/April

Setmana Santa (Holy Week): Palm branches are blessed in the island's churches on Palm Sunday and taken home to adorn balconies and front doors. Processions in Maó and Ciutadella on Good Friday.

June

Sant Joan (23–24 Jun): This is the most colourful of all Menorca's festivals, with traditions dating back to the Middle Ages. On the evening of 23 June there is a horseback procession around the Plaça des Born in Ciutadella, and on 24 June there are further processions, a Mass in the cathedral, jousting tournaments and finally a firework display in the Born. The celebrations get under way on the Sunday before 24 June (the Day of the Sheep), when a live lamb is carried around town on the shoulders of a man dressed in sheepskins.

July

Festa Patriòtica (9 Jul): A day of festivities in Ciutadella to commemorate the city's resistance against the Turkish attack in 1558.

La Verge del Carme (16 Jul): Processions of fishing boats in Maó, Ciutadella and Fornells in honour of the protector of fishermen.

Sant Martí (3rd weekend): Processions of horses, giants and Carnival figures in Es Mercadal.

Sant Jaume (24–26 Jul): Horseback parades and merriment in Es Castell.

Sant Antoni (4th weekend): Annual festivities in Fornells, including *jaleo* dancing on the waterfront.

August

Sant Cristòfol (early Aug): Es Migjorn Gran's annual festival features a 'blessing of the vehicles' by the parish priest.

Sant Llorenç (Sun after 10 Aug): *Caragols* dancing and prancing in the streets of Alaior.

Sant Bartomeu (23–25 Aug): Frolics in Ferreries, with cavalcades, music and dancing.

September

La Verge del Gràcia (7–9 Sep): Maó's main festival features cavalcades, street parties, donkey races, firework displays and regattas in the harbour.

December

Nadal (Christmas, 24–25 Dec): Midnight Mass is held in churches throughout Menorca.

Practical Matters

Above: *Ciutadella alleyway*
Below: *catching a siesta in Plaça des Born*

TIME DIFFERENCES

GMT 12 noon	Menorca 1PM	Germany 1PM	USA (NY) 7AM	Netherlands 1PM	Rest of Spain 1PM
→	→	→	←	→	→

BEFORE YOU GO

WHAT YOU NEED

●	Required	Some countries require a passport to remain valid for a minimum period (usually at least six months) beyond the date of entry – contact their consulate or embassy or your travel agent for details.	UK	Germany	USA	Netherlands	Spain
○	Suggested						
▲	Not required						
Passport/National Identity Card			●	●	●	●	▲
Visa			▲	▲	▲	▲	▲
Onward or Return Ticket			▲	▲	▲	▲	▲
Health Inoculations			○	○	●	○	○
Health Documentation (► 123, Health)			▲	▲	▲	▲	▲
Travel Insurance			○	○	○	○	○
Driving Licence (national with Spanish translation or International)			●	●	●	●	●
Car Insurance Certificate			●	●	●	●	○
Car Registration Document			●	●	●	●	○

WHEN TO GO

Menorca

■ High season
□ Low season

14°C	15°C	17°C	19°C	22°C	26°C	29°C	29°C	27°C	23°C	18°C	15°C
JAN	FEB	MAR	APR	MAY	JUN	JUL	AUG	SEP	OCT	NOV	DEC

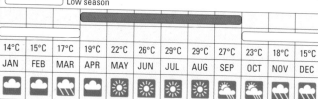

 Wet   Cloud   Sun   Showers/Sun

TOURIST OFFICES

In the UK
Spanish Tourist Office
22–3 Manchester Square
London W1M 5AP
☎ 020 7486 8077
Fax: 020 7486 8034
www.tourspain.es

In the USA
Tourist Office of Spain
666 Fifth Avenue 35th
New York
NY 10103
☎ 212/265 8822
Fax: 212/265 8864

Tourist Office of Spain
8383 Wilshire Boulevard
Suite 956
Beverly Hills
CA 90211
☎ 323/658 7188
Fax: 323/658 1061

POLICE (POLICÍA NACIONAL) 112 or 091

FIRE (BOMBEROS) 112

AMBULANCE (AMBULÀNCIA) 112 or 061

IN ANY EMERGENCY DIAL 112

WHEN YOU ARE THERE

ARRIVING

Spain's national airline, Iberia (☎ 971 36 90 15), has scheduled flights to Menorca from the Spanish mainland and major European and North American cities, but most visitors arrive by charter plane. Ferry services operate from Barcelona and Valencia on the Spanish mainland.

Maó (San Clemente) Airport to town centre	**Journey times**
5 kilometres	🚆 N/A
	🚌 N/A
	🚗 10 minutes

Maó Ferry Terminal to town centre	**Journey times**
	🚆 N/A
	🚌 N/A
	🚗 5 minutes

MONEY

The euro is the official currency of Spain. Euro banknotes and coins were introduced in January 2002. Banknotes are in denominations of 5, 10, 20, 50, 100, 200 and 500 euros and coins are in denominations of 1, 2, 5, 10, 20 and 50 cents, and 1 and 2 euros. Euro traveller's cheques are widely accepted, as are major credit cards. Credit and debit cards can also be used for withdrawing euro notes from cashpoint machines. Banks can be found in most towns in Menorca. Spain's former currency, the peseta, went out of circulation in early 2002.

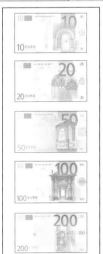

TIME

 Like the rest of Spain, Menorca is one hour ahead of Greenwich Mean Time (GMT+1), but from late March until late September, summer time (GMT+2) operates.

CUSTOMS

 YES
From another EU country for personal use (guidelines):
800 cigarettes, 200 cigars
1 kilogram of tobacco
10 litres of spirits (over 22%)
20 litres of aperitifs
90 litres of wine, of which 60 litres can be sparkling wine
110 litres of beer
From a non-EU country for your personal use, the allowances are:
200 cigarettes OR
50 cigars OR 250 grams of tobacco
1 litre of spirits (over 22%)
2 litres of intermediary products (e.g. sherry) and sparkling wine
2 litres of still wine
50 grams of perfume
0.25 litres of eau de toilette
The value limit for goods is 175 euros.
Travellers under 17 years of age are not entitled to the tobacco and alcohol allowances.

 NO

Drugs, firearms, ammunition, offensive weapons, obscene material, unlicensed animals.

CONSULATES

UK
☎ 971 36 33 73

Germany
☎ 971 36 16 68

USA
☎ 971 35 43 63

Netherlands
☎ 971 71 64 93

WHEN YOU ARE THERE

TOURIST OFFICES

**Tourist Board
(Foment del Turisme de
Menorca)**

● Carrer Nord 4
Maó
Menorca
☎ 971 36 23 77
Fax: 971 35 20 66
www.visitmenorca.com

**Tourist Information Centres
(Oficinas d'Informació
Turística)**

● Sa Rovellada de Dalt 24
Maó
Menorca
☎ 971 36 60 56
Fax: 971 36 74 15
Open: Mon–Fri 9–1, 3–7;
Sat 9–1

● Plaça de la Catedral
Ciutadella
Menorca
☎ 971 38 26 93
Fax: 971 38 26 67
Open: Mon–Fri 9–1:30, 5–7;
Sat 9–1

● Maó Airport
(inside arrivals terminal)
☎ 971 15 71 15
Open: Mar–Oct

Each office can supply you
with a free map of the
island plus information on
accommodation, places to
visit, beaches, buses, ferries,
car rental, etc.

NATIONAL HOLIDAYS

J	F	M	A	M	J	J	A	S	O	N	D
2		(1)	(1)	1(2)	(1)	1	1			1	1	3

1 Jan	New Year's Day
6 Jan	Epiphany
Mar/Apr	Good Friday, Easter Monday
1 May	Labour Day
May/Jun	Corpus Christi
25 Jul	Saint James' Day
15 Aug	Assumption of the Virgin
12 Oct	National Day
1 Nov	All Saints' Day
6 Dec	Constitution Day
8 Dec	Feast of the Immaculate Conception
25 Dec	Christmas Day

Shops, banks and offices close on these days but in
the main resorts many places remain open.

OPENING HOURS

○ Shops	● Churches
● Offices	● Museums
● Banks	● Pharmacies

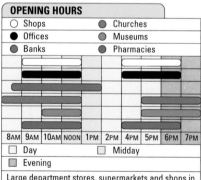

| 8AM | 9AM | 10AM | NOON | 1PM | 2PM | 4PM | 5PM | 6PM | 7PM |

□ Day	□ Midday
■ Evening	

Large department stores, supermarkets and shops in
tourist resorts may open outside these times,
especially in summer. In general, pharmacies, banks
and shops close on Saturday afternoon, though banks
stay open until 4:30PM Monday to Thursday, October
to May, but close Saturday, June to September.

The opening times of museums is just a rough guide;
some are open longer hours in summer while hours
are reduced in winter. Some museums close at
weekends and/or Monday.

DRIVE ON THE RIGHT

TOILETS FREE But hard to find. Use bars or supermarkets

PUBLIC TRANSPORT

 Inter-Island Flights Iberia operates several flights a day between Mallorca and Menorca (flight time: 30 minutes). There are no direct flights from Menorca to Ibiza (you are routed via Mallorca). Fares are inexpensive but you must book ahead at the height of summer (Iberia domestic flight reservations ☎ 902 40 05 00). For Maó airport information ☎ 971 15 70 00. (► 119, Arriving.)

 Buses Menorca has an extensive network of buses (operator: Transportes Menorca, ☎ 971 36 03 61) linking the towns of Maó and Ciutadella with most coastal resorts and interior villages, supplemented by more intermittent local services between smaller towns and neighbouring resorts. Destinations are marked on the front of the bus. Check the time of the last bus back. A timetable is published daily in the *Menorca* newspaper.

 Inter-island Ferries There are regular ferry services between Menorca and Mallorca. Trasmediterránea (☎ 971 36 60 50) operates a weekly car ferry between Palma and Maó (6 hours). There are also services twice daily between Ciudadella and Port d'Alcúdia on Mallorca with Iscomar (☎ 971 48 42 16). For day-trips to Mallorca, Cape Balear (☎ 902 10 04 44) have a passenger-only fast catermaran service to Cala Ratjada (1 hour) that departs twice daily from Ciutadella, making it possible to leave in the morning and return the same day. Cape Balear also offers organised day-trips on Thursdays, which combine a return boat ticket with a coach tour of Mallorca. Details and timetables for all these services can be found on page 2 of *Menorca* newspaper.

CAR RENTAL

 The leading international car rental companies have offices at Maó airport and you can book a car in advance (essential in peak periods) either direct or through a travel agent. Local companies offer competitive rates and will usually deliver a car to the airport.

TAXIS

 Taxis can be hired at ranks (indicated by a blue square with a 'T'), on the street (by flagging down those with a green light), or at hotels. They are good value within Maó but expensive over long distances. A list of tariffs is displayed at taxi ranks.

DRIVING

 There are no motorways. The only main road links Maó and Ciutadella (speed limit: **100kph**)

 Speed limit on minor roads: **40kph**

 Speed limit on urban roads: **60kph**

 Must be worn in front seats at all times and in rear seats where fitted.

 Random breath-testing. The blood-alcohol limit is 0.05%.

 All hire cars take either unleaded petrol (*sin plomo*) or diesel (*gasoleo*). There are 24-hour petrol stations in Maó, Ciutadella, Sant Lluís and on the C721 highway at Alaior and Es Mercadal. There are few petrol stations away from the main highway, though there is one close to Son Parc on the Maó to Fornells road. Most stations accept credit cards.

 If you break down driving your own car and are a member of an AIT-affiliated motoring club, you can call the Real Automóvil Club de España (☎ 915 93 33 33). If the car is hired follow the instructions given in the documentation; most of the international rental firms provide a rescue service.

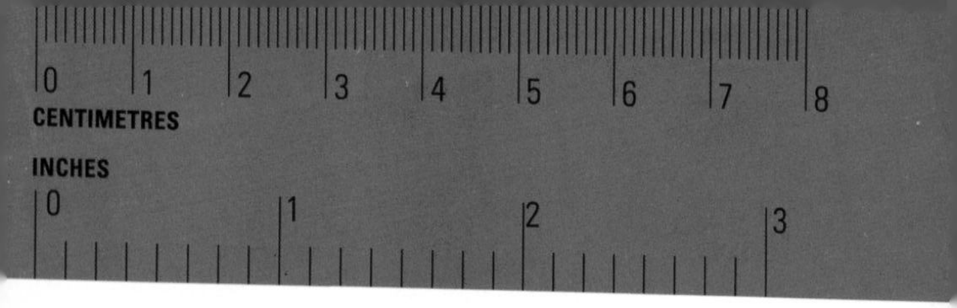

Ruler scale at top:
CENTIMETRES 0 1 2 3 4 5 6 7 8
INCHES 0 1 2 3

PERSONAL SAFETY

The national police force, the Policía Nacional (brown uniforms) keep law and order in urban areas. Some resorts have their own tourist-friendly Policía Turística. If you need a police station ask for *la comisaría*.

To help prevent crime:
- Do not carry more cash than you need.
- Do not leave valuables on the beach or poolside.
- Beware of pickpockets in markets, tourist sights or crowded places.
- Avoid walking alone in dark alleys at night.

Police assistance:
☎ **112**
from any call box

TELEPHONES

Most public telephones accept coins, credit cards and phonecards (*tarjetas telefónicas*), which can be bought at post offices, kiosks and *tabacos*.

All telephone numbers in the Balearic Islands have the same code (971), but within Menorca you still need to dial the full 9-figure numbers shown in this guide. To call the operator ☎ 002. For directory enquiries ☎ 003.

International Dialling Codes

From Menorca (Spain) to:

UK:	00 44
Germany:	00 49
USA:	00 1
Netherlands:	00 31

POST

Post Offices

Máo
✉ Carrer Bonaire 15
🕐 Mon–Sat 9–9
Ciutadella
✉ Plaça d'es Born 9
🕐 Mon–Fri 8:30–2:30, Sat 9:30–1
Stamps are also available from tobacconists and postcard shops.

ELECTRICITY

The power supply in Menorca is:
220–225 volts.

Sockets accept two-round-pin-style plugs, so an adaptor is needed for most non-Continental appliances and a transformer for appliances operating on 100–120 volts.

TIPS/GRATUITIES

Yes ✓ No ✗		
Restaurants (if service not included)	✓	10%
Cafés/bars	✓	change
Tour guides	✓	1 euro
Hairdressers	✓	1 euro
Taxis	✓	10%
Chambermaids	✓	1 euro
Porters	✓	1 euro
Theatre/cinema usherettes	✓	change
Cloakroom attendants	✓	change
Toilets	✗	

PHOTOGRAPHY

What to photograph: prehistoric monuments (*talayots*), secluded coves (*calas*), the old town areas of Maó and Ciutadella.

Best time to photograph: the Menorcan summer sun can be powerful at the height of the day making photos taken at this time appear 'flat'; it is best to photograph in the early morning or late evening.

Where to buy film: film and camera batteries are readily available from tourist shops and *drouguerías*.

HEALTH

Insurance
Nationals of EU and certain other countries can get medical treatment in Spain with the relevant documentation (Form E111 for Britons), although private medical insurance is still advised and is essential for all other visitors.

Dental Services
Dental treatment is not usually available free of charge as all dentists practice privately. A list of *dentistas* can be found in the yellow pages of the telephone directory. Dental treatment should be covered by private medical insurance.

Sun Advice
The sunniest (and hottest) months are July and August with an average of 11 hours sun a day and daytime temperatures of 29°C. Particularly during these months you should avoid the midday sun and use a strong sunblock.

Drugs
Prescription and non-prescription drugs and medicines are available from pharmacies (*farmàcias*), distinguished by a large green cross. They are able to dispense many drugs which would be available only on prescription in other countries.

Safe Water
Tap water is generally safe though it can be heavily chlorinated. Mineral water is cheap to buy and is sold as *con gas* (carbonated) and *sin gas* (still). Drink plenty of water during hot weather.

CONCESSIONS

Students Holders of an International Student Identity Card (ISIC) may be able to obtain some concessions on travel, entrance fees etc, but Menorca is not really geared up for students, it is more suited to families and senior citizens. There are no youth hostels, but for cheap accommodation there are two campsites near Cala Santa Galdana and Son Bou (► 103).

Senior Citizens Menorca is an excellent destination for older travellers, especially in winter when the resorts are quieter, prices more reasonable and hotels offer very economical long-stay rates. The best deals are available through tour operators who specialise in holidays for senior citizens.

CLOTHING SIZES

Menorca (Spain)	UK	Rest of Europe	USA		
46	36	46	36		
48	38	48	38		
50	40	50	40		
52	42	52	42		Suits
54	44	54	44		
56	46	56	46		
41	7	41	8		
42	7.5	42	8.5		
43	8.5	43	9.5		
44	9.5	44	10.5		Shoes
45	10.5	45	11.5		
46	11	46	12		
37	14.5	37	14.5		
38	15	38	15		
39/40	15.5	39/40	15.5		
41	16	41	16		Shirts
42	16.5	42	16.5		
43	17	43	17		
34	8	34	6		
36	10	36	8		
38	12	38	10		
40	14	40	12		Dresses
42	16	42	14		
44	18	44	16		
38	4.5	38	6		
38	5	38	6.5		
39	5.5	39	7		
39	6	39	7.5		Shoes
40	6.5	40	8		
41	7	41	8.5		

- Remember to contact the airport on the day prior to leaving to ensure the flight details are unchanged.
- If travelling by ferry you must check in no later than the time specified on the ticket.
- Spanish customs officials are usually polite and normally willing to negotiate.

LANGUAGE

The language that you hear on the streets is most likely to be Menorquín, a version of Catalan (Català), which itself shares features with both French and Spanish but sounds nothing like either and is emphatically a language, not a dialect. Catalan and Spanish both have official status on Menorca, and though Spanish will certainly get you by (it is still the language used by Menorcans to address strangers), it is useful to know some Catalan if only to understand all those street signs which are being slowly replaced in Catalan.

hotel	*hotel*	chambermaid	*cambrera*
bed and breakfast	*llit i berenar*	bath	*bany*
single room	*habitació senzilla*	shower	*dutxa*
double room	*habitació doble*	toilet	*toaleta*
one person	*una persona*	balcony	*balcó*
one night	*una nit*	key	*clau*
reservation	*reservas*	lift	*ascensor*
room service	*servei d'habitació*	sea view	*vista al mar*

bank	*banc*	credit card	*carta de crèdit*
exchange office	*oficina de canvi*	exchange rate	*tant per cent*
post office	*correus*	commission	*comissió*
coin	*moneda*	charge	
banknote	*bitllet de banc*	cashier	*caixer*
cheque	*xec*	change	*camvi*
traveller's cheque	*xec de viatge*	foreign currency	*moneda estrangera*

café	*cafè*	starter	*primer plat*
pub/bar	*celler*	main course	*segón plat*
breakfast	*berenar*	dessert	*postres*
lunch	*dinar*	bill	*cuenta*
dinner	*sopar*	beer	*cervesa*
table	*mesa*	wine	*vi*
waiter	*cambrer*	water	*aigua*
waitress	*cambrera*	coffee	*café*

aeroplane	*avió*	ticket	*bitlet*
airport	*aeroport*	single ticket	*senzill-a*
bus	*autobús*	return ticket	*anar i tornar*
station	*estació*	non-smoking	*no fumar*
bus stop	*parada*	car	*cotxe*
boat	*vaixell*	petrol	*gasolina*
port	*port*	how do I get to...?	*per anar a...?*
quay	*moll*	where is...?	*on és...?*

yes	*si*	you're welcome	*de res*
no	*no*	how are you?	*com va?*
please	*per favor*	do you speak English?	*parla anglès?*
thank you	*gràcies*		
welcome	*de res*	I don't understand	*no ho entenc*
hello	*hola*		
goodbye	*adéu*	how much?	*quant es?*
good morning	*bon dia*	open	*obert*
good afternoon	*bona tarda*	closed	*tancat*
goodnight	*bona nit*	today	*avui*
excuse me	*perdoni*	tomorrow	*demà*

INDEX

Acknowledgements
The Automobile Assocation wishes to thank the following libraries and photographers for their
assistance in the preparation of this book:
MARY EVANS PICTURE LIBRARY 10, 11; www.euro.ecb.int/ 119 (euro notes).

The remaining photographs are held in the Association's own library (AA PHOTO LIBRARY) and
were taken by JA TIMS, except:
R VICTOR f/cover b (cocktail); A BAKER f/cover e (palm tree).

Author's Acknowledgements
Tony Kelly would like to thank Señor Emilio de Balanzó of the Foment del Turisme de Menorca for
his kind assistance.

Contributors
Managing editor: Jackie Staddon Page Layout: Design 23
Indexer: Marie Lorimer